SanGita

စာ ஐ

The Harmony of Sanskrit and the Gita

A Primer on the Echoes of the Bhagavad Gita's Wisdom

Subi Subramanian

About this Book

॥ॐ॥

While many books on the Bhagavad Gita emphasize its philosophical teachings, this unique volume combines the beauty of Sanskrit with its profound wisdom, offering you deeper insights for a more enriching life. "SanGita" elegantly weaves together the philosophical principles of the Gita with the lyrical charm of Sanskrit, the world's oldest language.

Sanskrit, meaning "well-prepared," is celebrated for its poetic structure, particularly the Anuṣṭup chhandas, which enhances its musicality. Chanting the Gita in its original Sanskrit can enhance creativity, clarity of thought, concentration, and memory. The powerful shlokas transcend mere philosophy; in Sanskrit they have the potential to transform your perspective and guide you in your life.

This book not only reverberates with the wisdom of the Bhagavad Gita but also offers fresh interpretations of its Sanskrit terms. Understanding the text in its original language brings the classical Gita to life, enriching your reading experience.

Additionally, grasping the lineage and relationships among the Pandavas and Kauravas is essential for a deeper understanding of the Gita's characters and context. The author carefully explains these connections while highlighting the aesthetic and intellectual allure of Sanskrit, making the text more engaging and meaningful.

The Sanskrit verses have been shown to enhance cognitive function, promote spiritual growth, and instill a sense of discipline. Investing your time and resources in this book is highly recommended for anyone seeking a transformative experience.

Contents

1 Author's Preface

वसुदेव सुतं देवं, कंस चाणूर मर्दनम् ।
देवकी परमानंदं, कृष्णं वंदे जगद्गुरुम् ॥ 1 ॥

Vasudeva-Sutaṁ Devaṁ Kaṁsa-Cāṇūra-Mardanam
Devakī-Paramānandaṁ Kṛṣṇaṁ Vande Jagadgurum

I salute the world's guru Krishna, the son of Vasudeva,
Who killed Kamsa and Chanura, and the source of great joy to Devaki

— Verse from Krishnashtakam of Sri Adi Sankaracharya

My Journey with Sanskrit and the Bhagavad Gita

Namaste! As a school student in Pune, I was fortunate to immerse myself in the study of Sanskrit and the Bhagavad Gita, experiences that profoundly shaped my understanding of its teachings. In recent years, I've had the privilege of sharing this knowledge through teaching Sri Rudram, Sanskrit, and various ancient Indian scriptures. Encouraged by friends and students, I launched "Easy Sanskrit," a series of learning sessions that later transitioned online, enabling me to connect with learners around the globe.

Many have expressed a desire to delve deeper into the Sanskrit terminology within the Bhagavad Gita. The structure of Sanskrit, along with its rich intellectual tradition and cultural significance, renders it a unique vessel for conveying profound knowledge and spiritual wisdom. Inspired by this realization, I sought to explore the Bhagavad Gita through the lens of the Sanskrit language, celebrating its beauty and depth.

This journey led to the creation of 'SanGita,' an online program that harmonizes the elegance of Sanskrit with the philosophy of the Gita. To ensure accessibility for students unfamiliar with the Devanagari script, I designed slides featuring verses in both Devanagari and their English transliteration. The positive feedback was overwhelming, with many students expressing gratitude for the clarity and insight gained during our sessions.

This book serves as a summary of the SanGita online program, encapsulating twenty sessions that I hope will resonate with readers. The Bhagavad Gita embodies the essence of the Vedas, offering timeless wisdom that is universally applicable. It provokes thought and provides practical guidance for leading a fulfilling life, offering solace to those in distress. As the immortal song of the Lord, it invites us to appreciate the beauty of existence and encourages us to strive for a better life.

In response to my online programs, I have received countless messages of appreciation from individuals around the world. These heartfelt notes have inspired me to compile this book, and I extend my deepest thanks to everyone who has motivated me to think, create, and give back with love. I am pleased to include some of this feedback as a testament to our shared journey.

It is my sincere hope that readers find this book both accessible and enriching. In closing, I wish to express my profound gratitude to my dear friend Sri K. Raman, whose patience and support were invaluable in compiling this work.

Thank you for joining me on this journey.

Subi Subramanian   E-mail: gurujisubi@gmail.com
Chicago

Feedback on my online programs

Namaskaram Sir!

It is really enjoyed listening and learning from you. The videos are excellent, short, clear and the flow between them is maintained well. I can see up to session 9 uploaded in YouTube and curious to know if there are more. Do you conduct online courses? If so, please provide details for me to enroll.

As a yogin, understanding the meanings of all words in the shlokas is a wonderful experience for me. I speak about 12 languages and clearly see that all are derived from Sanskrit. Truly a treasure which sadly many of us Indians especially the younger generations are missing out on. Pranaam

(Dr.) Tanuja Halady, Lausanne, Switzerland

Dear Sir,

Greetings and Pranaam. I came across your channel on Youtube while searching for Sanskrut through English and Gita lessons.

Its great listening to you and seeing your videos. The presentation style and explanation of every word and its context and cross references that you draw, along with past narratives style is superb and captivating. Its making learning a fun based activity which one looks forward to, feel spell bound to hear one session after the other.

Thank you, Sir, for this crisp presentation style, your efforts are like making an animation film, where tremendous efforts required to make, but outcome appears so child friendly.

Thanks sir, Pranaam once again.

Warm Regards,
Minoo Shah
24 Frames Digital, Mumbai

Dear Sir,

I am a senior citizen of seventy-two, and I must say without any hesitation that Prof. Subramanian's method of teaching Sanskrit is inspiring and attractive, and at this age I did not fall into sleep!

Vasudevan D, India

Priya Sriman Subramanyaha,

Namo namaha! I have been following your YouTube videos on "Easy Sanskrit" up to the first 4 lessons but without the slides and have found them fascinating and very instructive and illuminating. However, after the first 4 lessons I am stuck and cannot proceed further.

Therefore, following your advice in the comments section of the video, I would like to enroll for your weekly lessons with the slides in order to get the full benefit of your brilliant teaching.

If I may introduce myself, I am a 88 year old retired senior Indian Navy officer currently living in the USA with my daughter. I have actually studied Samskrutam in school and college more than 70 years ago but sadly, due to my service in the Navy, I have lost touch with this wonderful basha though I can still broadly follow the meanings of the various slokams, stotrams and suktams I recite daily. Listening to your teaching brings back to me what I learnt a long time ago. For this I thank you.

Namaskaram

Commodore (Rtd) K.S. Subramanian
California

Dear Guruji,

Namonamah!

I listened to the SanGita 7 with joy. I am learning a lot the way you combine the Sanskrit teaching, the meaning, and SanGita. Today, as I woke up, I wanted to listen to Sri Rudram, one of my favorite prayers. Soon, I realized how easier it is to hear the pronunciation and the sound that dresses each word. Even from distance, say in the kitchen, I was able to hear clearly! Wow! How lovely it is to be able to have that. This is partly due to your generous heart full with love for teaching this essential lesson to us and the mankind. My eyes followed with ease the Devanagri scripts and I was and am so grateful to you. How little, I knew that your class with such dear content, the whisper of divine song could help me with lovely Sri Rudram hearing!

I have your blessings and Bhagavan's Grace together that all this is possible. Thank you dear Guruji!

I loved the way you said that Lord Krisna had just one disciple like Arjuna... who was definitely chosen by the Lord to be the candidate of humanity for humankind. Saying this, I would like to add that your role as a Guru propagating the Lord's message is precious to our heart; I am ever grateful for it.

I love Bhagavad Gita so much for it literally weaves a royal road to divinity for one and all, especially for those who are tired of all brutality in physical and astral reality. I thank you so much again and again for your love and practice of this most ancient custom of living you share with us with so much care and love. Please, keep doing what you are doing...without these lessons or jewels life feels barren.

P.S. Please, share this newsletter with others if you see the need.

Please take care Guruji. With Gratitude and love.

Hari Aum,
Zahra Nafez
Los Angeles, California

Harih Om Guruji,

Sir, I am 60 years, living in Pune. I knew you are from Pune when, one of your early lectures, you mentioned how a humble Maharashtrian says "Kasha Kay Ram Ram" :)

I have followed 3 lessons of yours online, but I am unable to recite anywhere close to how you do. I am an ardent follower of Adi Sankara since past 20 years or so.

Sir I am very keen to learn Shri Rudra. Even if my lungs don't permit proper chanting, at least it will give me the pleasure of learning.

I reconnected with Sanskrit after almost 45 years, about 9 months ago. Attended a Sambhashana Shibir of Samskrita Bharati and am now able to speak a few sentences, with a lot of grammatical errors no doubt. But I love it and am enjoying the experience, especially the fact that I am able to understand Bhagavad Gita better than ever before :)

Kindly let me know when I can join your class. I look forward to learning both Sanskrit and Shri Rudra from you.

With love and regards. Pranaams

Kamal Kothari
Pune, India

2 Sanskrit + Gita – "SanGita"

Preamble: In the pages that follow, the slides that were presented at the online 'SanGita' sessions are reproduced. Each verse is in Sanskrit and in English to help those who are not proficient in reading the Devanagari script. We begin with an explanation of the SanGita program, its objectives, proposed approach, and an introduction to the Bhagavad Gita.

2.1 Welcome to SanGita Program!

Enjoy the beauty of Sanskrit words and the philosophy of Bhagavad Gita

2.2 Objectives of SanGita Program

Combine Sanskrit + Bhagavad Gita learning to:

- Upgrade your knowledge of Sanskrit through Gita

- Experience the intrinsic power of Sanskrit words

- Enjoy the beauty of Sanskrit verses

- Improve your pronunciation of Sanskrit words

- Bring a new perspective to life through this primer on Gita

- Develop a positive outlook and get guidance

- Strengthen mind management for happy life

2.3 Approach to SanGita Program

- Like earlier "Easy Sanskrit" program

- Online learning sessions of Sanskrit and Gita together

- Frequency: Once a week - every Saturday morning

- Duration of each session - about one hour

- Methodology: Through visuals coupled with commentaries on Sanskrit and Bhagavad Gita

- Prior knowledge of Sanskrit/Devanagari script is helpful

2.4 Introduction to Bhagavad Gita

- Song of Bhagawan – the Lord (It is not called Krishna Gita!)

- Found in Bhisma-Parva, in Mahabharata, a great Epic said to be dictated by Sri Veda Vyasa and written by Ganesha

- A dialogue between Lord Krishna and Arjuna on a battlefield at Kurukshetra

- A core sacred text of Sanatana Dharma and its philosophy

- Gita is also known as **'Gitopanishad.'**

Essence of Bhagavad Gita

The essence of Bhagavad Gita is explained in the following beautiful verse:

राजविद्या राजगुह्यं पवित्रमिदमुत्तमम 1
प्रत्यक्षावगमं धर्म्यं सुसुखं कर्तुमव्ययम 11

rāja-vidyā rāja-guhyaṁ pavitram idam uttamam

pratyakṣhāvagamaṁ dharmyaṁ su-sukhaṁ kartum avyayam

(Chapter 9 - Verse 2 of Bhagavad Gita)

The King of all Wisdom, The King of all Secrets, The Purest and the Best

Provides a direct perception of the 'Self' by realization within oneself

The Perfect Religion, Everlasting in Happiness and Joyfully performed

---

Author's Note on Sanskrit Usage in this book

A knowledge of Sanskrit or Devanagari script is very helpful to understand the verses in Bhagavad Gita. To help readers who are not conversant with Sanskrit, the book provides transliteration of Sanskrit Verses in English. The nearest meanings of Sanskrit words are also given in English.

To understand some grammatical aspects of Sanskrit, some words are marked with alphabetic abbreviations such as R (Root), Gender M (Masculine), F (Feminine), N (Neuter), Tense and Vibhakti (Case).

There are many long words in the Sanskrit verses making it difficult for pronunciation and understanding. The long words are made up of small words by joining them. The joint is called 'Sandhi.' संधि (Sandhi) is a combination of two sound-elements.

For example: नमः + ते = नमस्ते, एतत् + श्रुत्वा = एतत्छ्रुत्वा

There are three types of Sandhis in Sanskrit.

1. स्वर संधि (Swara Sandhi): Joins similar sounds आ + अ, कदा + अपि = कदापि; इ + ई, रवि Ravi + इंद्र Indra = रविन्द्र Ravindra

2. व्यंजन संधि (Vyanjana Sandhi): consonant with another consonant or a vowel. एतत् + श्रुत्वा = एतत्छ्रुत्वा, अस्मिन् + अरण्ये = अस्मिन्नरण्ये,

3. विसर्ग संधि (Visarga Sandhi): Replace त or स with स् after विसर्ग like नमः + ते = नमस्ते, . इतः + ततः = इतस्तत

First step in understanding long words in Sanskrit is segregation of the components of combined word by पदच्छेद (padacheta) or splitting up.

When you go through the verses, you will find some long words are split up to make it not only easier for understanding but also to appreciate the beauty of Sanskrit.

For better understanding of Bhagavad Gita, a reader must know the lineage and the relationships of the families involved in the mighty war between the Kauravas and Pandavas. To help the readers, the author has included dynasty charts of the of Kuru Vamsam and the Yadu clan.

Enjoy reading this book!

Dynasty Chart

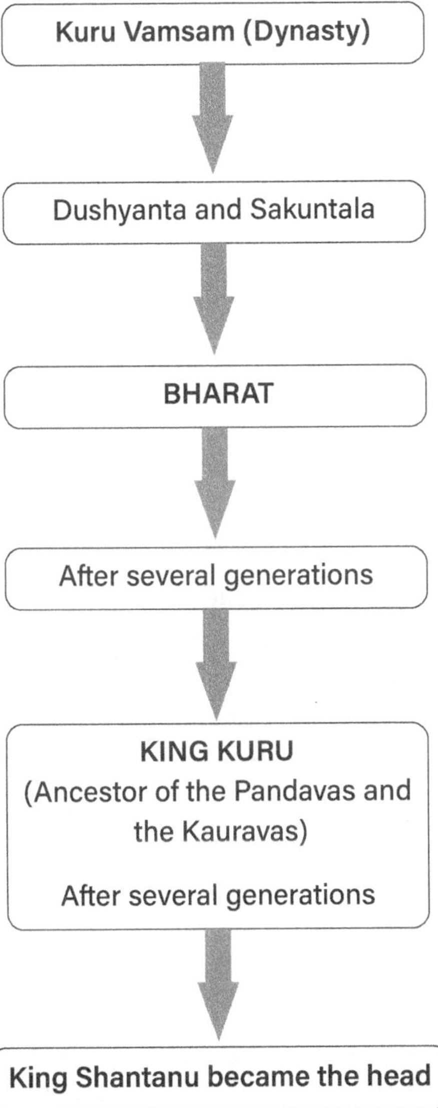

The Kuru Family Chart

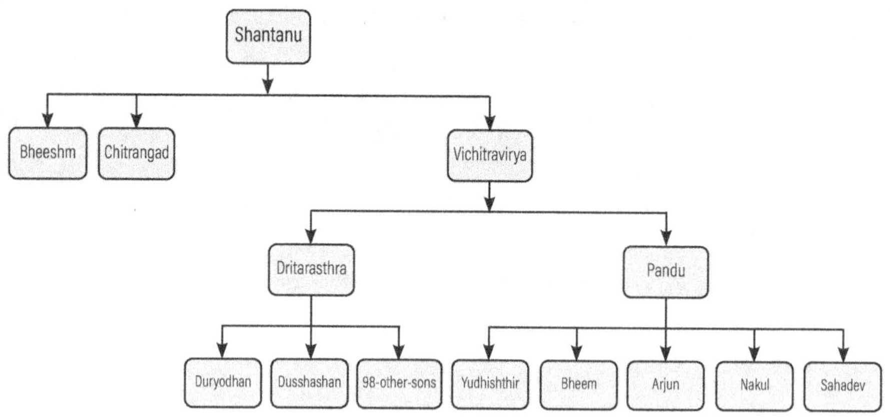

The Yadu Dynasty

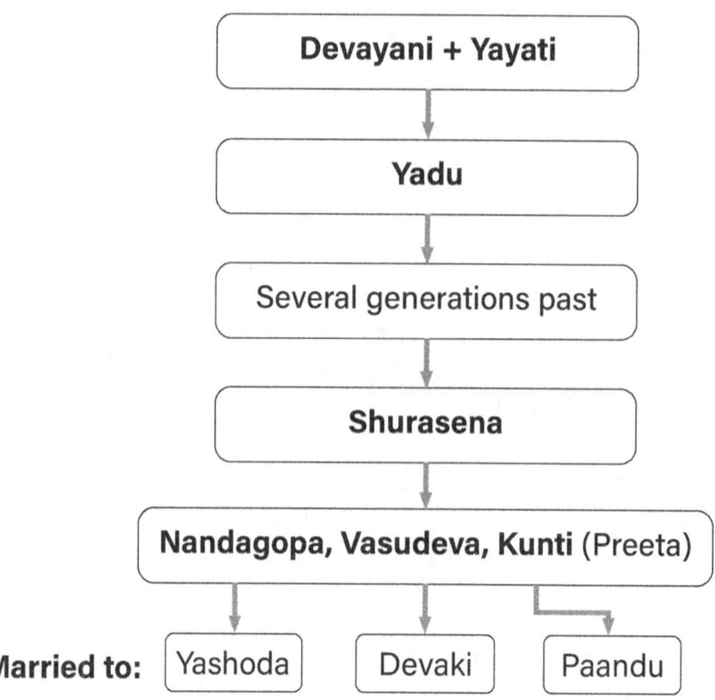

Krishna born to Vasudeva and Devaki as an incarnation of Lord Vishnu

- Krishna showed Himself as Lord Vishnu at birth

- Performed many miracles as a child

- A Super Charmer with multiple divine qualities - **Kalyana Gunas**

- Unique Avataram of Lord Vishnu, called as **Poorna Avataram**

- Known as **'Jagadguru'**

Background to Bhagavad Gita

Dhritarashtra and Pandu were brothers. Dhritarashtra married Gandhari, while Pandu had Kunti and Madri as wives. Due to a curse, Pandu could not be with his wives, but Kunti, using a boon from a sage, had three sons—Yudhisthira, Bhima, and Arjuna—while Madri had twins, Nakula and Sahadeva, through celestial beings. Dhritarashtra fathered a hundred sons, the Kauravas. After Pandu's death, the Pandavas were raised alongside the Kauravas.

As they grew up, jealousy from Duryodhana, the Kaurava leader, led to a rigged dice game in which Yudhisthira lost everything, including Draupadi. The Pandavas were forced into thirteen years of exile. Afterward, they sought their rightful share of the kingdom, but Duryodhana refused. With encouragement from Kunti and Krishna, the Pandavas prepared for war.

Both sides approached Krishna for support. Arjuna chose Krishna as his charioteer, prioritizing spiritual guidance over military strength. Duryodhana chose Krishna's army. Krishna attempted to mediate peace but was rejected by Duryodhana, who even tried to imprison Him. Krishna revealed His divine form to Dhritarashtra, who, despite his attachment to his sons, could not prevent the impending war.

Before the battle, Veda Vyasa granted Sanjaya the ability to see and report the events of the war to the blind king Dhritarashtra, who preferred to hear about the battle rather than see the destruction of his family.

Bhagavad Gita Contents

- 18 Chapters containing 700 verses
- The Essence of Vedas
- Divided into three Yogas

  1. **Karma Yoga** – The path of proper actions
  2. **Bhakti Yoga** – The path of proper devotion
  3. **Gnana Yoga** – The path of self-enquiry or *'Atma Vichaara'*

The Beauty of Chandas in Sanskrit: Chandas refers to the poetic meter or rhythm used in classical Sanskrit literature. It plays a crucial role in the composition and structure of verses. There are several types of Chandas, each with its own specific rules.

Some well-known chandas (meters) include:

Anuṣṭup: A common meter consisting of 32 syllables, typically used in many verses of the Bhagavad Gita and other texts.

Trishtubh: Composed of 44 syllables, often used in classical poetry.

Gāyatrī: A 24-syllable meter that is significant in Vedic hymns.

Chandas is an essential part providing the aesthetic and musical qualities to Bhagavad Gita. Most verses in the Gita are set to the *anushtubh chandas (*meter), with 4 lines of 8 syllables each.

Selected Dhyana Slokams (Meditative Prayers)

Dhyana Slokam-1

Sri Adi Shankaracharya's Dhyana Shloka

पार्थाय प्रतिबोधितां भगवता नारायणेन स्वयम्

व्यासेन ग्रहिताम् पुराणमुनिना मध्ये महाभारते 1

अद्वैतामृत वर्षिणीं भगवतीं अष्टादशाध्यायिनीम्

अम्बा त्वां अनुसन्दधामी भगवद् गीते भव द्वेषिनीं ॥

pārthāya pratibodhitāḿ bhagavatā nārāyaṇena svayaḿ

vyāsena grathitāḿ purāṇa-muninā madhye mahābhārate

advaitāmṛta-varṣiṇīḿ bhagavatīm aṣṭādaśādhyāyinīḿ

amba tvām anusandadhāmi bhagavad-gīte bhava-dveṣiṇīm

Meaning

O Bhagavad-gita, thou hast been instructed to Arjuna, the son of Prtha by the Lord Himself and afterwards thee were included within the Mahabharata by the ancient sage Vyasa. Thy eighteen divine chapters rain upon us, the immortal nectar of the wisdom of the Absolute. O mother, destroyer of man's rebirth into the darkness of this mortal world, upon thee I meditate.

Dhyana Slokam-2

मूकं करोति वाचालं पङ्गुं लङ्घयते गिरिं ।

यत्कृपा तमहं वन्दे परमानन्द माधवम् ॥

mūkaṁ karoti vācālaṁ paṅguṁ laṅghāyate girim

yat-kṛpā tam ahaṁ vande paramānanda-mādhavam

Meaning

The dumb speak with eloquence and the lame cross the high Mountains,

I remember and extol the Grace that flows from the Supreme manifestation of Madhava.

3 Srimad Bhagavad Gita

॥ श्रीमद्भगवद्गीता ॥

अथ प्रथमोऽध्यायः । Chapter 1
अर्जुन विषादयोगः

The Yoga of the Despondency of Arjuna

Verse 1.1

धृतराष्ट्र उवाच ।

धर्मक्षेत्रे कुरुक्षेत्रे समवेता युयुत्सवः ।

मामकाः पाण्डवाश्चैव किमकुर्वत संजय ।।१-१।।

Dhritaraashtra Uvaacha:

Dharmakshetre kurukshetre samavetaa yuyutsavah;

Maamakaah paandavaashchaiva kim akurvata sanjaya. 1-1

Explanation to Verse 1.1

धृतराष्ट्रः - Dhritarashtra: King of Hastinapura उवाच - to speak धृतराष्ट्रं - धृतः to hold or bear. राष्ट्रं - nation, kingdom धर्मक्षेत्रे - धर्मस्य क्षेत्रम् - field where righteousness prevails The first verse of Bhagavad Gita starts with Dharma!

कुरु क्षेत्रे - कुरू णां क्षेत्रम् - The field of Kurus समवेताः - सम् + अव + इ - to descend together युयुत्सवः - युध् + आ - युयुत्सु - one who desires to fight मामकाः - मम + **suffix** क - showing affection like बालः **&** बालकः पाण्डवाः sons of Paandu च and एव also, all किम् what अकुर्वत कृ - to do - *Past tense* Akurvata

What did the sons of Pandu and my people do, assembled, eager to fight on the holy field of Kurukshetra, O Sanjaya?

Commentary - Verse 1.1

The very first Shloka of the Bhagavad Gita begins with "Dharma". What is Dharma? That which is good for all species. One that sustains and upholds righteous living.

Sastras prescribe four different pursuits for mankind - Dharma, Artha, Kama, Moksha. Dharma is the first Purushaartha –The Hindu religion is called Sanaatana (Eternal) Dharma.

The Holy Bhagavad Gita – the song of the Divine starts in a battlefield. In the earliest Krita Yuga, the war was fought between two worlds – the Asura and Devas. In Treta Yuga, the war was between two countries – Rama Raj (India) and Ravana's Lanka. In Dvapara Yuga, the battle was between two related families – the Kauravas and the Pandavas. In Kali Yuga, the battle is really within oneself – the good and the evil, dharma (righteousness) and adharma that includes undesirable temptations and destructive desires.

The first verse in Bhagavad Gita starts with a very simple question from king Dhritarashtra (meaning one who supports/bears the nation). Dhritarashtra asks, "What did my sons do?" Dhritarashtra is blind and he is asking this question. Like him, many people are blind when they search for Truth. So, likewise, people need to ask questions to search and discover the Truth.

Whom does the king ask? He is asking Sanjay, his charioteer, who at that time has become his eyes to the world. Sanjay is the one who is about dispel the darkness by explaining the events as they progress. But who is Sanjay? A mere charioteer? NO. He has been given the Divine sight to see the distant event – like a TV – like you are able to see me even though you are located far off. Sanjay is telling us about the dialogue through his divine insight. King Dhritarashtra is asking the first question to Sanjay to describe "What did my dear sons do?" It is only then he continues to say, "what did the sons of Pandu do?" Dhritarashtra calls the sons of Pandu and not 'my nephews" or the sons of my dear brother. He is so indifferent to his brother Pandu whose death brought him the Kingdom. He loves his sons even though they were totally inconsiderate to his brother's sons. It is said that when Bhima comes before him after the great war, Krishna places the blind king before a stone image of Bhima knowing how much anger is built up in the King. Dhritarashtra does not even realise that he is embracing a stone and squeezes it so hard that it crushed into pieces!

The very first lesson of the Bhagvad Gita is anger and hate will lead to destruction, and it is essential to practice and acquire mental equilibrium in our lives.

Verse 1.2

संजय उवाच ।

दृष्ट्वा तु पाण्डवानीकं व्यूढं दुर्योधनस्तदा ।

आचार्यमुपसंगम्य राजा वचनमब्रवीत् ।।१-२।।

Sanjaya Uvaacha:

Drishtwaa tu paandavaaneekam vyudham duryodhanastadaa;
Aachaaryam upasamgamya raajaa vachanam abraveet. 1-2

Explanation to Verse 1.2

संजय = सम् + जि - he who wins, name of the charioteer of धृतराष्ट्र दृष्ट्वा - Having seen - by whom? by दुर्योधनः -the eldest son of धृतराष्ट्र: - दुर्योधनः = दुष्कर - difficult + युध् to fight - one who is hard to fight against पाण्डवानीकम् = पाण्डवा + अनीकम् - the army of Pandavas व्यूढम् - वि + ऊह् - to set in formation of army – phalanx. तदा - then, *(a conjunction)* आचार्यम् = आ + चर् to conduct oneself - म् - to teacher *(second vibhakti singular)* उपसंगम्य = उप + सम् + गम् - to go near राजा - King; वच् - to tell - वचनम् - word or saying

Sanjaya said, "Seeing the Pandava's army arranged in a formation, King Duryodhana went over to Acharya (Dronacharya) and said:

Commentary Verse 1.2

Seeing the Pandava army arranged in a 'vyudam' that means 'phalanx' - a way of mass military formation usually composed of heavy infantry, King Duryodhana went near his Acharya (preceptor) who was the brahmin commander-in-chief and said these words. Duryodhana means 'one who is hard to fight with.' As an experienced soldier, he surveyed the strength of the enemy's army. For a king, there was no need to go near the commander, but Duryodhana had a specific purpose in doing so.

Verse 1.3 Introduction of Warriors

पश्यैतां पाण्डुपुत्राणां आचार्य महतीं चमूम् ।

व्यूढां द्रुपदपुत्रेण तव शिष्येण धीमता ।।१-३।।

Pashyaitaam paanduputraanaam aachaarya mahateem chamoom;

Vyoodhaam drupadaputrena tava shishyena dheemataa 1.3

Explanation to Verse 1.3

पश्य, एतां - to see (V), this, पाण्डु-पुत्राणां - sons of Paandu (P) आचार्य - refers to Dronacharya – the family Guru महतीम् - *adjective,* comes from महत् - large (F) चमूम् from चमू (R) referring to army (F); व्यूढाम् - set in army formation (F) द्रुपदपुत्रेण - by द्रुपदपुत्र - son of Drupada, called by the name Dhristudyumnan

तव - you – your; शिष्येण - शिष्य - disciple धीमता - intelligent (A) धीमत् - धीमत् = धी intellect + मत् (धीः अस्य अस्ति)

Acharya, see this vast army of sons of Paandu, arranged in formation by your intelligent disciple and son of King Drupada.

Commentary 1.3

Dronacharya was the teacher to both the Kauravas and Pandavas. He and King Drupada, father of Draupadi, studied together and were friends in their younger days. Later King Drupada insulted poor Dronacharya and they became enemies. Despite being enemies, Dronacharya taught archery to Dhristadyumna, son of King Drupada. Now, in this battlefield, Dhristadyumna, Dronacharya's student, is supporting the Pandavas. It was he who arranged the army's formation. Besides, Arjuna of the Pandavas was one of Dronacharya's favorite students. Dronacharya was facing his own best students who have gathered to fight against him. So, Duryodhana makes a sarcastic remark to Dronacharya – your intelligent disciple, the son of Drupada. He hints to Dronacharya not to be lenient to the enemies that includes his best students. Apparently, Duryodhana is unnerved by the strength of the enemy.

Verse 1.4

अत्र शूरा महेष्वासा भीमार्जुनसमा युधि ।
युयुधानो विराटश्च द्रुपदश्च महारथः ।।१-४।।

Atra Shoora Maheshvaasaa Bheemarjunasamaayudhi
Yuyudhaano viraatascha drupadascha mahaaratha: 1.4

Explanation to Verse 1.4

अत्र - here, *(conjunction)*; शूरा: - brave, heros (A, M, P) महान् इष्वास: यस्य स: = महेष्वास: Having big bows (P, M) भीम: - भी: fear + म: has not - one who has no fear अर्जुन: - faultless भीम: च अर्जुन: च = भीमार्जुन: सम: - equal युधि - युध् **(R)** & आ - to fight युयुधान: विराट: च - Yuyudhana and Virata द्रुपद: - King Drupada महारथ: having a large chariot – a title given to great kings (A)

Here are heroes, mighty archers, equal in battle to Bhima and Arjuna, Yuyudhana, Virata and Drupada, of the great chariot.

Commentary 1.4

In the army of the Pandavas, there were many other well-known warriors who can fight fiercely.

Duryodhana knew well the mighty strength of Bhima and Arjuna and so, he compares other warriors with them.

Verse 1.5

धृष्टकेतुश्चेकितानः काशिराजश्च वीर्यवान् ।
पुरुजित्कुन्तिभोजश्च शैब्यश्च नरपुंगवः ॥१-५॥

Dhrishtaketush chekitaanah kaashiraajashcha veeryavaan;
Purujit kuntibhojashcha shaibyashcha narapungavah. 1.5

Explanation to Verse 1.5

धृष्टकेतु: = धृष्ट: केतु: येन स: - a king who fought with Ketu चेकितान: - King Chekitana; काशिराज: King of Kaashi (M, S) वीर्यवान् - the Brave – *adjective* P, पुरुजित् - who won King Puru कुन्ति: भोग: यस्य स: - one who enjoyed Kunti's kingdom and hence, called कुन्तिभोज: - Adopted father of Kunti शैब्य: - descendant of King Shibi – well-known for charity नरपुङ्गवः = नरेषु पुङ्गवः - the best amongst men (A to Shaibya)

Drishtaketu, Chekitana and the valiant king of Kaashi, Purujit, Kuntibhoja and Shaibya, the best of men.

Verse 1.6

युधामन्युश्च विक्रान्त उत्तमौजाश्च वीर्यवान् ।

सौभद्रो द्रौपदेयाश्च सर्व एव महारथाः ।।१-६।।

Yudhaamanyushcha vikraanta uttamaujaashcha veeryavaan;
Saubhadro draupadeyaashcha sarva eva mahaarathaa: 1.6

Explanation to Verse 1.6

युधामन्युः - Name of a warrior; Derived from युधा -War मन्युः-Angry यस्य सः He who is = who becomes angry by war; विक्रान्तः - वि + क्रम् **(R)** display valor उत्तमौजा: A warrior's name - उत्तमं ओजस् यस्य सः = who has shine of brilliance; सौभद्र: - son of Subhadra; द्रौपदेया: - sons of Draupadi (क्रमशः प्रतिविन्ध्य, सुतसोम, श्रुतकर्मा, शतानीक और श्रुतसेन:); सर्वे - all, एव - too, even महारथाः(A) – a title for great warriors

The brave Yudhamanyu, Uttamaujas, the son of Subhadra (Abhimanyu, the son of Arjuna), and the sons of Draupadi, all of them too are great warriors

Commentary 1.5 & 1.6

Duryodhana speaks out the names of the warriors who are great heroes, each having a history of success in the battlefield.

Verse 1.7

अस्माकं तु विशिष्टा ये तान्निबोध द्विजोत्तम ।

नायका मम सैन्यस्य संज्ञार्थं तान्ब्रवीमि ते ।।१-७।।

Asmaakam tu vishishtaa ye taan nibodha dwijottama;
Naayakaah mama sainyasya samjnaartham taan braveemi te 1.7

Explanation to Verse 1.7

अस्माकम् - *pronoun of first person* अस्मद् *plural* – ours तु - also; विशिष्टाः - वि + शिष् - best or specially (vishesha) ये who (those), तान् those, निबोध know (thou), द्विजोत्तम - द्वि Two, जायते - जन्(R) to be born उत्तमः best (O) best among the twice-born, नायकाः - leaders, मम -my, सैन्यस्य - of the army, संज्ञार्थम् - सम्यक् Summary अर्थः meaning - FYI, तान् - them, ब्रवीमि - ब्रू(R) - speak, tell ते - to you.

Know also, O best among the twice-born (refers to Brahmin who is said to be born again as Brahmachari at the Upanayanam), the names of those most distinguished amongst ourselves, the leaders of my army! I tell you this for your information.

Verse 1.8

भवान् भीष्मश्च कर्णश्च कृपश्च समितिंजयः ।
अश्वत्थामा विकर्णश्च सोमदत्तिस्तथैव च ।। १- ८।।

Bhavaan bheeshmashcha karnashcha kripashcha samitinjayah;
Ashwatthaamaa vikarnashcha saumadattis tathaiva cha 1.8

Explanation to Verse 1.8

भवान् - *second person respectful 'you'* (M, S) भीष्मः - Bheeshma – fearless - drawn from भी (R) – fear, च - and (C) कर्णः - Karna, कृप:- Krupa समितिंजयः Samithinjayah -Victorious अश्वत्थामा - Ashwattaama – son of Dronacharya विकर्णः - Vikarna; सोमदत्तिः Somadatti – son of Somadatta (Jayadratha). All names of best warriors तथा एव च and likewise

Thyself and Bhisma, and Karna and Kripa, the victorious in war; Asvatthama, Vikarna, and Jayadratha, the son of Somadatta

Commentary 1.7 & 1.8

For the information of Dronacharya, Duryodhana provides a briefing about the valorous captains who are exceptionally qualified to lead his army.

Verse 1.9

अन्ये च बहवः शूरा मदर्थे त्यक्तजीविताः ।
नानाशस्त्रप्रहरणाः सर्वे युद्धविशारदाः ॥ १- ९॥

Anye cha bahavah shooraa madarthe tyaktajeevitaah;
Naanaashastrapraharanaah sarve yuddhavishaaradaah.

Explanation to Verse 1.9

अन्ये - Other (P) च and (C) बहवः - many शूरा -brave (A, M) मदर्थे - मम अर्थः - for my purpose त्यक्तजीविताः = त्यज् **R**, त्यक्तम् - to sacrifice, जीविताः life नाना - many varied शस्त्र -weapons प्रहरणा striking (from R- प्र to strike) सर्वे - all युद्ध - war विशारदाः skilled

And many other heroes who risk their lives for my sake, armed with a variety of weapons and all skilled in warfare.

Verse 1.10

अपर्याप्तं तदस्माकं बलं भीष्माभिरक्षितम् ।
पर्याप्तं त्विदमेतेषां बलं भीमाभिरक्षितम् ॥ १-१० ॥

Aparyaaptam tad asmaakam balam bheeshmaabhirakshitam;
Paryaaptam twidam eteshaam balam bheemaabhirakshitam. 1.10

Explanation to Verse 1.10

अपर्याप्तम् - unlimited, (परि + आप् -to limit), तत् - that, अस्माकम् - ours, बलम् – strength भीष्माभिरक्षितम् - marshaled by Bhisma, *(Past tense S)*, तु

but, however (C), इदम् - this, पर्याप्तं - limited, एतेषाम् - this (army) भीमाभिरक्षितम् - marshalled by Bhima

That strength of our army marshalled by Bhisma is unlimited whereas their army, marshalled by Bhima, is limited.

Commentary 1.10

In this verse, Duryodhana makes a comparative assessment of his army with that of Pandavas. He feels his army is much stronger as it is marshalled by Grandfather Bhisma who is the most experienced general. In contrast, Pandava's army is marshalled by Bhima who is junior to Bhisma and much less experienced. Duryodhana feels overconfident that his army will be victorious.

Verse 1.11 Duryodhana Instructs His Army

अयनेषु च सर्वेषु यथाभागमवस्थिताः ।

भीष्ममेवाभिरक्षन्तु भवन्तः सर्व एव हि ॥ १-११ ॥

Ayaneshu cha sarveshu yathaabhaagam avasthitaah;

Bheeshmam evaabhirakshantu bhavantah sarva eva hi. 1-11

Explanation to Verse 1.11

अयनेषु - अय् (R) to go or come च - and (C), सर्वेषु सर्व - all, यथाभागम् - as divided/assigned, अवस्थिताः =अव + स्था इति -having been at a place, भीष्ममेवा -भीष्मम् (Vibhakti 2, S), + एव - only अभिरक्षन्तु - To take care, (V क्रियापदम्), भवन्तः you (P)

Therefore, you all, having been assigned your respective (strategic) positions in the army, take care of Bhisma only.

Commentary 1.11

Having realized the high importance of Bhisma in this war, Duryodhana instructs all his soldiers to support Bhisma and protect him fully without leaving their assigned strategic positions.

Verse 1.12 Bhisma Blows the Conch

तस्य सञ्जनयन्हर्षं कुरुवृद्धः पितामहः ।

सिंहनादं विनद्योच्चैः शङ्खं दध्मौ प्रतापवान् ॥ १-१२॥

Tasya sanjanayan harsham kuruvriddhah pitaamahah;

Simhanaadam vinadyocchaih shankham dadhmau prataapavaan. 1-12

Explanation to Verse 1.12

तस्य - तत्+अस्य - his, सञ्जनयन् = सम्+जन्- One who arouses, हर्षम्- happy, कुरु-वृद्धः Kuru – Old - वृध् (R) - old among Kurus (M, S), पितामहः - grand-father, सिंह-नादम्-Lion roar, विनद्य = वि + नद्" – give out a call, उच्चैः - loudly, शङ्खम् - Conch, दध्मौ - blow, प्रतापवान् = प्रतापः अस्य अस्ति – valorous

His (Duryodhana's) excited and valorous grandfather Bhisma, the elder amongst the Kauravas, now roared like a lion and blew his conch to give out a war call.

Commentary 1.12

Bhisma, the oldest of the Kuru dynasty, the mighty grandfather, blew the conch like the roar of a lion. In the battlefield, like in sports, the soldiers need to be cheered up to fight. The sound from the conch induces a cheerful spirit, particularly in the mind of King Duryodhana. It also signifies the declaration of war against the Pandavas.

Verse 1.13 The War Cry Starts

ततः शङ्खाश्च भेर्यश्च पणवानकगोमुखाः ।

सहसैवाभ्यहन्यन्त स शब्दस्तुमुलोऽभवत् ॥ १-१३ ॥

Tatah shankhaashcha bheryashcha panavaanaka gomukhaah;
Sahasaivaabhyahanyanta sa shabdas tumulo'bhavat 1-13

Explanation to Verse 1.13

ततः - then (C) शङ्खाः - conches (P, M), च - and (C) , भेर्यः P arising from भेरि (F) Kettle drums, पणवाः च आनकाः च गोमुखाः च = पणवानकगोमुखाः - tabors, large military drums and instruments shaped like cow-horn, सहसा - suddenly, अभ्यहन्यन्त = अभि + हन् - to beat in order to make sound, शब्दः noise, तुमुलः - tumultuous,(*see the similarity between Sanskrit and English*) अभवत् - to be

Then, conches and kettledrums, tabors, drums and cow-horns blared forth suddenly (from the Kauravas); making tumultuous sound (war-cry!)

Commentary 1.13

The blowing of conch by grandsire Bhisma is followed by a thunderous noise created by the Kaurava warriors using a combination of instruments including conches, kettledrums, tabors, trumpets, and cow-horns. Such a great noise sets the vibrant mood for initiating the fight.

Verse 1.14 Pandavas respond to the war cry

ततः श्वेतैर्हयैर्युक्ते महति स्यन्दने स्थितौ ।

माधवः पाण्डवश्चैव दिव्यौ शङ्खौ प्रदध्मतुः ॥ १-१४ ॥

Tatah shvetair hayair yukte mahati syandane sthitau;
Maadhavah paandavashchaiva divyau shankhau pradadhmatuh 1-14

Explanation to Verse 1.14

ततः - then, श्वेतैः - white (A), हयैः - horses P of हय - horse (M), युक्ते - yoked – (*from the R* युज् *-to join*), महति - large (A) – *from* महत्, स्यन्दने - to chariot स्यन्दन, स्थितौ – seated माधवः - a name for Krishna (clan of madhu, consort of MA), पाण्डवः - Pandava, दिव्यौ =दिव् १ - to shine, divine, शङ्खौ - two conches (D), प्रदध्मतुः ="प्र + ध्मा" - to blow

Then, also Madhava, and the son of Pandu (Arjuna), seated in their magnificent chariot yoked with white horses, blew their divine conches

Commentary 1.14

This verse describes the response of the Pandavas to the Kauravas. Madhava is another name for Lord Krishna. Pandava – meaning son of Pandu – refers to Arjuna here. The Chariot used by Arjuna was a gift of Lord Agni (fire) to Arjuna. The conches used by Krishna and Arjuna are described as divine (*Divyow- see similarity with Divine*). Using such divine articles and the support of Lord Krishna (an avataram of Lord Vishnu) indicates victory to the Pandavas.

Verse 1.15 Blowing Divine Conches

पाञ्चजन्यं हृषीकेशो देवदत्तं धनञ्जयः ।

पौण्ड्रं दध्मौ महाशङ्खं भीमकर्मा वृकोदरः ॥ १-१५॥

Paanchajanyam hrisheekesho devadattam dhananjayah;

Paundram dadhmau mahaashankham bheemakarmaa vrikodarah 1-15

Explanation to Verse 1.15

पाञ्चजन्यं - name of conch हृषीकेशो -of Hrishikesa meaning Krishna देवदत्तं conch of धनञ्जयः - Arjuna । पौण्ड्रं - name of conch दध्मौ - blow महाशङ्खं -

big conch of Bhima, भीमकर्मा - one who frightens others वृकोदरः = वृक + उदरः - *Wolf, hyena + belly* - one, who has a belly like a वृक wolf (refers to Bhima)

Conches too had names. Hrishikesa (Krishna) blew the "Panchajanya" and Arjuna blew the "Devadatta", and Bhima, the doer of terrible deeds, (having a slim belly like a wolf) blew the great conch, "Paundra".

Commentary 1.15

In the Bhagavad Gita, Lord Krishna is called by different names, and so is Arjuna. In this verse, Krishna is called Hrishikesa as He is the master of the mind and senses. The term Dhananjaya (Dhanam plus Jaya) means one who is the conqueror of wealth. It refers to Arjuna as he conquered hidden wealth from many rulers and made use of it for various yagnas (sacrifices) and public welfare. The conches too have names. Krishna blew the conch called Panchajanya while Arjuna used the conch named Devadatta.

Vrikodhara – meaning who has the belly of a wolf – refers to Bhima.

Wolf is a terrible beast known for eating voraciously but it has a concave stomach, and not bulging out. Bhima had similar traits and hence called Vrikodhara. His conch is called Paundra.

Verse 1.16 Pandava Brothers Blow Conches

अनन्तविजयं राजा कुन्तीपुत्रो युधिष्ठिरः ।

नकुलः सहदेवश्च सुघोषमणिपुष्पकौ ॥ १-१६ ॥

Anantavijayam raajaa kunteeputro yudhishthirah;

Nakulah sahadevashcha sughosha manipushpakau 1-16

Explanation to Verse 1.16

अनन्तविजयम् - name of conch-shell of युधिष्ठिरः YudhiShtira, राजा -king, कुन्तीपुत्रः - son of Kunti, नकुलः सहदेवश्च , Nakula and Sahadeva, सुघोष , मणिपुष्पकौ - 'Sugosha,' 'Manipushpakow' names of conch-shells of Nakula and Sahadeva respectively

Yudhisthira, the son of Kunti, blew the "Anantavijaya"; and Sahadeva and Nakula blew the "Manipushpaka" and "Sughosha" conches.

Commentary 1.16

Yudhistra, the eldest of the Pandava brothers, is described here as the son of Kunti and a Raja. He is also known as Dharmaputra, the son of Dharma. He exhibits graceful qualities as a king, though not wearing a crown. The verse gives the names of conches used by him and by Nakula and Sahadeva.

Verse 1.17 Introducing Shikandi

काश्यश्च परमेष्वासः शिखण्डी च महारथः ।

धृष्टद्युम्नो विराटश्च सात्यकिश्चापराजितः ॥ १-१७॥

Kaashyashcha parameshwaasah shikhandee cha mahaarathah;
Dhrishtadyumno viraatashcha saatyakishcha aparaajita 1-17

Explanation to Verse 1.17

काश्याः - of Kashi, च - **and**, परमेष्वासः = परमः + इष्वासः supreme bow, शिखण्डी – one having a tuft, महारथः title, धृष्टद्युम्न: - son of Drupada, विराट: King Virata, अपराजितः - undefeated, सात्यकि: - name of warrior

The king of Kashi, an excellent archer with the supreme bow, Shikandi, the mighty warrior, Dhristadyumna and Virata and Satyaki, the undefeated,

Commentary 1.17

Among the supporters of the Pandavas was the King of Kasi, an excellent archer. Shikandi was an eunuch who had sworn that he will kill Bhisma. There is a long story behind it. In short, Shikhandi was a princess named Amba in previous birth. She was abducted by Bhisma and later spurned by him due to his celibacy vow. Bhisma had sworn that he will not fight against a woman or an enunuch. So, eventually, Shikandi became the cause of Bhisma's defeat.

Dhristadyumna, son of Drupada, is one who cannot be easily defeated. Virata and Satayaki are supporting kings who are unconquered.

Verse 1.18 Other Warriors Join the War-Cry

द्रुपदो द्रौपदेयाश्च सर्वशः पृथिवीपते ।

सौभद्रश्च महाबाहुः शङ्खान्दध्मुः पृथक्पृथक् ॥ १-१८ ॥

Drupado draupadeyaashcha sarvashah prithiveepate;

Saubhadrashcha mahaabaahuh shankhaan dadhmuh prithak prithak 1-18

Explanation to Verse 1.18

द्रुपदः - name of king of Panchal(father of Draupadi*i*), द्रौपदेया: sons of द्रौपदी, सर्वशः all as such, पृथिवीपते – पृथिवी(Earth) + पते (Lord), Lord of the earth, king, सौभद्रः "सौभद्र" - son of सुभद्रा -Abhimanyu, महाबाहुः - having big arms, शङ्खान्दध्मुः - blew their conches (P), पृथक्पृथक् - respectively

Drupada, Lord of the Earth (King) and the sons of Draupadi, and the son of Subhadra, the mighty-armed, all blew their respective conches!

Commentary 1.18

Sanjaya is addressing Dhritarashtra as 'Prithivipate' meaning, 'O, Ruler of the Earth' thus giving him the highest importance. He indicates that now the war is about to begin with Drupada, the sons of Draupadi and the might Subadhra have blown their conches.

Verse 1.19 Impact of Noise on Kauravas

स घोषो धार्तराष्ट्राणां हृदयानि व्यदारयत् ।

नभश्च पृथिवीं चैव तुमुलोऽभ्यनुनादयन् ॥ १-१९॥

Sa ghosho dhaartaraashtraanaam hridayaani vyadaarayat;
Nabhashcha prithiveem chaiva tumulo vyanu naadayan. 1-19

Explanation to Verse 1.19

स घोषो - that loud sound, धार्तराष्ट्राणाम् - people of धृतराष्ट्र, हृदयानि - hearts (N) व्यदारयत् - Tore व्यदारयत् - वि + दारृ (R) १० - to tear, नभः - Sky, च - and, पृथिवीम् - the Earth, एव - also, तुमुलः - tumultuous, व्यनुनादयन् - (वि + अनु + नद् - *to resound*), reverberating

The tumultuous sound tore the hearts of Dhritarashtra's party, reverberating between heaven and earth.

Commentary 1.19

The battle scene is set to be scary for the Kauravas with the tumultuous uproar caused by the Panadava group members blowing their conches. The reverberating noise pierced the hearts of Kauravas, called here as Dhritarashtras. Duryodhana was scared as it often happens with a person having a guilty mind.

Verse 1.20 Arjuna picks up the bow

अथ व्यवस्थितान्दृष्ट्वा धार्तराष्ट्रान् कपिध्वजः ।
प्रवृत्ते शस्त्रसम्पाते धनुरुद्यम्य पाण्डवः ॥ १-२० ॥
हृषीकेशं तदा वाक्यमिदमाह महीपते ।

Atha vyavasthitaan drishtwaa dhaarta raashtraan kapidhwajah;

Pravritte shastra sampaate dhanurudyamya paandavah 1-20

Hrisheekesham tadaa vaakyamidamaaha maheepate;

Explanation to Verse 1.20

अथ - So, and then, व्यवस्थितान् - to settle down, दृष्ट्वा - seeing, धार्तराष्ट्रान् - party of Dhritarashtarah, कपिध्वजः - one having monkey *(refers to Hanuman)* on his flag, प्रवृत्ते - प्र + वृत्+१ आ - to begin, शस्त्रसंपाते - clash of arms, धनुः - bow, उद्यम्य - to pick up, पाण्डवः -Arjuna, हृषीकेशम् - to Krishna, तदा - then, वाक्यम् sentence, इदम् - this, आह - to say, महीपते -O, Lord of the Earth

Then, seeing all the people of Dhritarashtra's party settled and the clash of weapons about to begin, Arjuna, the son of Pandu, whose ensign was that of a monkey, picked up his bow and said this to Krishna O Lord of the Earth – (reports Sanjay)

Commentary 1.20

Now, everything is set for the war to start. When the shooting of arrows was to commence, Arjuna with the monkey insignia (Hanuman banner) saw the Kauravas arrayed. (Hanuman signifies courage and victory). Arjuna lifted the bow (to signify a hold) and spoke thus to Krishna.

Verses 1.21 and 1.22

अर्जुन उवाच ।
सेनयोरुभयोर्मध्ये रथं स्थापय मेऽच्युत ॥ १-२१ ॥

यावदेतान्निरीक्षेऽहं योद्धुकामानवस्थितान् ।

कैर्मया सह योद्धव्यमस्मिन् रणसमुद्यमे ॥ १-२२॥

Arjuna Uvaacha:

Senayor ubhayormadhye ratham sthaapaya me'chyuta. 1-21

Yaavad etaan nireekshe'ham yoddhukaamaan avasthitaan; Kair mayaa saha yoddhavyam asmin ranasamudyame 1-22

Explanation to Verses 1.21 and 1.22

अर्जुन उवाच - Arjuna Said सेनयोरुभयोर्मध्ये - split to सेनयो: उभयो: Two armies मध्ये - center (षष्ठी *V dual*) रथं Chariot, स्थापय *to Park* मेऽच्युत - अच्युतः Krishna (**च्युतः** *to fall*) यावत् - until, एतान् - this, निरीक्षे - निर् + ईक्ष् १- to observe, अहम् – I योद्धुकामान् - desiring to fight, अवस्थितान् - अव + स्था - to set into order, कै: -किम् - what, मया - my, सह - with, योद्धव्यम् - to fight, अस्मिन् - this, रण-समुद्यमे - battle undertaken together

In the middle of the two armies, park my chariot, O Krishna, so that I may see those who stand here, desirous to fight, and know with whom I must fight when the battle begins.

Verse 1.23

योत्स्यमानानवेक्षेऽहं य एतेऽत्र समागताः ।

धार्तराष्ट्रस्य दुर्बुद्धेर्युद्धे प्रियचिकीर्षवः ॥ १-२३॥

Yotsyamaanaan avekshe'ham ya ete'tra samaagataah; Dhaartaraashtrasya durbuddher yuddhe priyachikeershavah 1-23

Explanation to Verse 1.23

योत्स्यमानाः – *split to* ये योत्स्यन्ते ते - Those who will fight (*future particple of* युध् -*to fight*) अवेक्षे = अव + ईक्ष् - to perceive, observe, अहं ,ये एते, अत्र I, those, there, समागताः – split to सम् + आ + गम् - came together (*Plural, Past tense*), दुर्बुद्धे: - दु: + बुद्धिः (दुष् *R- bad*), -one with crooked mind, युद्धे

- in battle, प्रिय-चिकीर्षवः = (कर्तुं इच्छुः चिकीर्षुं) - wishing to please, derive pleasure, धार्तराष्ट्रस्य - the son of Dhritashtra - Duryodhana

For I desire to observe those who are assembled here to fight, wishing to please in battle, Duryodhana, the crooked-minded son of Dhritashtra

Commentary 1.21, 1.22 & 1.23

Arjuna addresses Krishna as *Achyuta* – one of the significant names of Vishnu (*you will find it in Vishnu Sahasranamam-the thousand names of Vishnu*) - meaning one who is unfailing, unchangeable (the glorious one). He asks Krishna, the driver of his chariot, to park the chariot between the two armies so that he may clearly see the Kaurava soldiers with whom he must fight. Arjuna also wants to see the kings who are supporting the evil-minded (*durbudheh*) Duryodhana.

Verse 1.24 Sanjaya Speaks

सञ्जय उवाच ।

एवमुक्तो हृषीकेशो गुडाकेशेन भारत ।

सेनयोरुभयोर्मध्ये स्थापयित्वा रथोत्तमम् ॥ १-२४॥

Sanjaya Uvaacha
Evamukto hrisheekesho gudaakeshena bhaarata;
Senayor ubhayormadhye sthaapayitwaa rathottamam 1-24

Explanation to Verse 1.24

एवमुक्तो - एवम् + उक्तः thus, spoken to हृषीकेशो – Krishna गुडाकेशेन - (गुडा-*sleep*; गुडाकायाः - निद्रायाः, तस्याः ईशेन) - *who has forsaken sleep, ever-alert; Adj. for Arjuna,* भारत - a descendant of King भरत (Dhritarashtra), सेनयोरुभयोर्मध्ये - between the two armies, स्थापयित्वा -placed firmly रथोत्तमम् -the best of chariots

Being thus addressed by Arjuna, Lord Krishna, having stationed the best of chariots, O Dhritarashtra, in the midst of the two armies, ...

Verse 1.25

भीष्मद्रोणप्रमुखतः सर्वेषां च महीक्षिताम् ।

उवाच पार्थ पश्यैतान्समवेतान्कुरूनिति ॥ १-२५॥

Bheeshmadronapramukhatah sarveshaam cha maheekshitaam;
Uvaacha paartha pashyaitaan samavetaan kuroon iti. 1-25

Explanation to Verse 1.25

भीष्मद्रोणप्रमुखतः = भीष्मः च द्रोणः च - Bhisma and Drona प्रमुखतः - facing सर्वेषां - **all** च **and** महीक्षिताम् - महीं क्षयति - Earth rulers (Kings), उवाच पार्थ - said, O Partha (Arjuna) पश्यैतान्समवेतान्कुरूनिति – split to पश्य + एतान् + समवेतान् + कुरून् + इति - see +these +gathered together + Kurus (*descendants of Kuru*) + so

In front of Bhisma and Drona and all the rulers of the earth, (Krishna) said so: "O Partha (Arjuna), see now all these Kurus gathered together!"

Krishna earned the name as 'Parthasarathy' as he served as the Sarathy (chariot driver) to Partha (Arjuna). There is a temple for him in Triplicane, Chennai. Lord Krishna has a moustache here, as he was born as a Kshatriya in the Yadhava Dynasty. As a charioteer, the Lord adorned a moustache (as a symbol of dignity and wisdom). So, he is also known as Meesai-Perumal (God with a moustache) in Tamil.

Commentary 1.24-1.25

Sanjaya continues to provide the commentary on the battle scene. Arjuna is described as Gudakeshah. Gudaka refers to the tamasic quality of being sleepy, dull or lazy. Ishah means master. So, the expression Gudakeshah means who has overcome sleepiness or mastered dullness. He is ever-alert. As asked by Arjuna, Krishna placed the chariot in between the armies in front of great warriors like Bhisma and Drona and asked Arjuna to see the Kauravas, the descendents of Kuru (includes the Pandavas too). Arjuna is addressed here as Partha – son of Pritha.

The lesson here is one should overcome dullness and be always alert to become of master of skills like Arjuna.

Verse 1.26 Arjuna's Sorrow

तत्रापश्यत्स्थितान्पार्थः पितृनथ पितामहान् ।

आचार्यान्मातुलान्भ्रातृन्पुत्रान्पौत्रान्सखींस्तथा ॥ १-२६ ॥

Tatraapashyat sthitaan paarthah pitrin atha pitaamahaan; Aachaaryaan maatulaan bhraatrun putraan pautraan sakheemstathaa 1-26

Explanation to Verse 1.26

तत्रापश्यत्स्थितान्पार्थः - तत्र -there अपश्यत् saw स्थितान् stood पार्थः Partha *(Arjuna)*, पितृनथ - पितृ, father + अथ also पितामहान् - grandfather, आचार्यान् - acharyas मातुलान् - maternal uncles *(Mathulan and maternal sound similar)* भ्रातृन् - brothers **(word Bratha similar to Brother)** पुत्रान् -sons पौत्रान् -grandsons सखीन् friends, तथा -also

Then Arjuna saw there stationed, grandfathers and fathers, teachers, maternal uncles, brothers, sons, grandsons and friends, too.

Verse 1.27

श्वशुरान्सुहृदश्चैव सेनयोरुभयोरपि ।

तान्समीक्ष्य स कौन्तेयः सर्वान्बन्धूनवस्थितान् ॥ १-२७ ॥

कृपया परयाविष्टो विषीदन्निदमब्रवीत् ।

Shvashuraan suhridashchaiva senayorubhayorapi;

Taan sameekshya sa kaunteyah sarvaan bandhoon avasthitaan 1-27

Kripayaa parayaa'vishto visheedannidam abraveet;

Explanation to Verse 1.27

श्वशुरान् fathers-in-law, सुहृद:- =(सुष्ठु हृद् यस्य सः) well-wishers सेनयोरुभयोरपि - in between the armies, तान्समीक्ष्य = तान् तत् that, समीक्ष्य - सम् + ईक्ष् - observe, कौन्तेयः- son of Kunti सर्वान्बन्धूनवस्थितान् = सर्व + बन्धु + अवस्थितान् - all relatives stationed, कृपया - compassion, परया – extreme आविष्ट: pity विषीदन् sorrowfully इदम् thus अब्रवीत् spoke

(He saw) fathers-in-law and friends also in both armies. The son of Kunti, Arjuna, seeing all these kinsmen standing arrayed, spoke thus sorrowfully, filled with deep pity.

Commentary 1.26-1.27

On seeing his close relatives including Grandfather Bhisma and cousins, acharyas who taught him warfare, and others, Arjuna is overcome with emotion.

According to ancient Hindu tradition, five people are to be respected as fathers. First one is *janitaa,* the biological father, the second is *upanethaa,* one who performs the upanayanam ceremony and gives the sacred thread, the third is the Guru who teaches, the fourth is *annadhaata,* the one who provides food and lastly, *bhaya thraata,* one who saves your life in case of a grave danger. Brothers of one's biological father are also considered equivalent to one's own father. So, Arjuna is looking here at many fathers – though not biological. In some religions, even a priest is called a father.

The great warrior Arjuna who raised his bow, now saw his opponents and other warriors as merely relatives, teachers and well-wishers (*shrushtu hrudyah:* with good hearts). Looking at them, Arjuna feels sad, and gets choked with attachment *(krupaya, also referred as raagah)* and supreme compassion *(paraya krupaya)*. He seems to have lost his sense of duty as a Kshatriya warrior. This loss of *vivekam* (discrimination) is born out of ignorance and signifies a serious challenge to him. Deep emotion plays a major role in the lives of human beings.

Verses 1.28 and 1.29

अर्जुन उवाच ।

दृष्ट्वेमं स्वजनं कृष्ण युयुत्सुं समुपस्थितम् ॥ १-२८॥

सीदन्ति मम गात्राणि मुखं च परिशुष्यति ।

वेपथुश्च शरीरे मे रोमहर्षश्च जायते ॥ १-२९॥

Arjuna Uvaacha:

Drishtwemam swajanam krishna yuyutsum samupasthitam 1-28

Seedanti mama gaatraani mukham cha parishushyati;
Vepathushcha shareere me romaharshashcha jaayate 1-29

Explanation to Verses 1.28 and 1.29

दृष्ट्वा -Having seen इमम् -**this** स्वजनम् - relatives युयुत्सुं desirous of fighting समुपस्थितम् assembled, सीदन्ति fail, मम गात्राणि my limbs मुखं mouth च and परिशुष्यति dries up, वेपथुश्च trembling, शरीरे मे body, my रोमहर्षश्च जायते - hair stands on end

Seeing these, my kinsmen, O Krishna, arrayed, eager to fight, my limbs fail and my mouth is parched up, my body trembles and my hairs stand on end!

Commentary 1.28 & 1.29

Now Arjuna tells his feelings of sorrow to Krishna. The result of attachment or raagah is often sokah – sorrow. If any object of deep attachment is lost or damaged, the result is often sadness or sorrow that shows up in body language as lamenting, shouting or crying.

At first, Arjuna talks about his physical condition. Seeing his kinsmen assembled there, he feels weakness overpowering him as his limbs fail, and mouth gets parched. It happens to people who are stuck with deep distress. Arjuna is thus stressed with his body shaking, hairs standing on end (horripulation), the bow Gaandeevam slipping from his hands, and the skin feeling a burning sensation.

Lesson: Anything of deep attachment causes misery, if it is lost. The body language shows it.

Verse 1.30

गाण्डीवं स्रंसते हस्तात्त्वक्कैव परिदह्यते ।

न च शक्नोम्यवस्थातुं भ्रमतीव च मे मनः ॥ १-३० ॥

Gaandeevam sramsate hastaat twak chaiva paridahyate;

Na cha shaknomyavasthaatum bhramateeva cha me manah 1-30

Explanation to Verse 1.30

गाण्डीवम् - name of Arjuna's bow (N), स्रंसते - slips हस्तात् -from hand (M, Vibhakti 5), त्वक् - skin, एव- also, परिदह्यते,= परि + दह् -heats up, न शक्नोमि - not able to अवस्थातुम् - to stand, भ्रमतीव- भ्रम् (R) reeling च **and (C)** मे मनः my mind

The Gandiva (bow) slips from my hand and my skin burns all over; I am unable even to stand, my mind is reeling, as it were.

Commentary 1.30

Unable to even stand, Arjuna continues to lament. He addresses Krishna as *Keshava- the destroyer of demon Kesin.* Keshav has other meanings like one having beautiful hair on his head. It is also a word that combines the letters K for Brahma, the creator, A for Vishnu, the sustainer, and Isha – referring to Rudra, the destroyer. Arjuna feels his mind is unsteady. He starts imagining many strange things.

The strong relationship between the body and the mind is demonstrated here. The weakness of the mind reveals itself through various reactions on his body. *The emotions show up in body language. If we observe carefully, we can witness body language every day in others.* Arjuna continues to describe his mind and body reactions in the next few verses.

Verse 1.31

निमित्तानि च पश्यामि विपरीतानि केशव ।

न च श्रेयोऽनुपश्यामि हत्वा स्वजनमाहवे ॥ १-३१ ॥

Nimittaani cha pashyaami vipareetaani keshava;

Na cha shreyo'nupashyaami hatwaa swajanam aahave 1-31

Explanation to Verse 1.31

निमित्तानि - Omens (P), च पश्यामि **and** I see विपरीतानि - Bad, केशव - O Keshava (Krishna) न **no** च **and** श्रेयोऽनुपश्यामि - श्रेयः अनुपश्यामि see any benefit, हत्वा -in killing, स्वजन -my own people (kith and kin), आहवे - in battle

And I see bad omens, O Kesava! I do not see any benefit in killing my kinsmen in battle.

Verse 1.32

न काङ्क्षे विजयं कृष्ण न च राज्यं सुखानि च ।

किं नो राज्येन गोविन्द किं भोगैर्जीवितेन वा ॥ १-३२ ॥

Na kaangkshe vijayam krishna na cha raajyam sukhaani cha;

Kim no raajyena govinda kim bhogair jeevitena vaa 1-32

Explanation to Verse 1.32

न काङ्क्षे neither desire विजयं victory कृष्ण O Krishna न **nor** च राज्यं kingdom सुखानि pleasures च and **(C)** किं - what नो of राज्येन the kingdom, गोविन्द =गो cows विन्दति tends इति गोविन्दः One who tends cows- refers to Krishna, भोगैर्जीवितेन वा = भोगैः *(from R भुज् to enjoy)* enjoyments, जीवितेन - life, वा - even

For I desire neither victory, O Krishna, nor pleasures nor kingdom! Of what avail is a kingdom to us, O Govinda, or enjoyments or even life?

Commentary 1.31-1.32

Arjuna tries to justify his thoughts saying he sees bad omens. He tells Krishna that fighting this war is futile as he feels nothing good will come out of it. He is perplexed and indifferent to victory and material pleasures gained by winning the war. Addressing Krishna as Govinda, he asks Krishna of what use is winning the kingdom or enjoyment or even life. Arjuna expects Krishna to agree with his reasoning.

Verse 1.33

येषामर्थे काङ्क्षितं नो राज्यं भोगाः सुखानि च ।
त इमेऽवस्थिता युद्धे प्राणांस्त्यक्त्वा धनानि च ॥ १-३३॥

Yeshaam arthe kaangkshitam no raajyam bhogaah sukhaani cha;
Ta ime'vasthitaa yuddhe praanaamstyaktwaa dhanaani cha 1-33

Explanation to Verse 1.33

येषामर्थे - For whose sake काङ्क्षितं- we desire नो राज्यं - kingdoms भोगाः- enjoyments सुखानि -pleasures च -**and** त इमेऽवस्थिता - they stand here

युद्धे - in battle प्राणांस्त्यक्त्वा having renounced (left behind) their lives धनानि च and wealth

Those for whose sake we desire kingdoms, enjoyments and pleasures, stand here in battle, having renounced life and wealth

Verse 1.34

आचार्याः पितरः पुत्रास्तथैव च पितामहाः ।

मातुलाः श्वशुराः पौत्राः श्यालाः सम्बन्धिनस्तथा ॥ १-३४॥

Aachaaryaah pitarah putraastathaiva cha pitaamahaah;
Maatulaah shwashuraah pautraah shyaalaah sambandhinas tathaa

Explanation to Verse 1.34

आचार्याः -teachers पितरः -fathers पुत्रास्तथैव - also sons च पितामहाः - and grand fathers मातुलाः - maternal uncles श्वशुराः-fathers-in-law पौत्राः - grand sons श्यालाः -brothers-in-law सम्बन्धिनस्तथा - likewise 'relatives' bonded by marriage (The Sanskrit word for "bond" is bandham. See the similarity. सम्बन्धि is derived from it)

Teachers, fathers, sons and grandfathers, grandsons, fathers-in-law, maternal uncles, brothers-in-law and relatives by marriage.

Commentary 1.33-1.34

He feels distressed seeing his teachers, fathers (as explained before, brothers and cousins of biological father are also considered as fathers), grandfathers, uncles, sons, grandsons, in-laws, and a host of other relatives who stand there for the battle staking their lives and property. In every war, the soldiers who fight may lose their lives or get injured for the sake of their country. Arjuna feels sorry for these soldiers and does not want to be responsible for their destruction.

Verse 1.35

एतान्न हन्तुमिच्छामि घ्नतोऽपि मधुसूदन ।

अपि त्रैलोक्यराज्यस्य हेतोः किं नु महीकृते ॥ १-३५॥

Etaan na hantum icchaami ghnato'pi madhusoodana;

Api trailokya raajyasya hetoh kim nu maheekrite 1-35

Explanation to Verse 1.35

एतान्न हन्तुमिच्छामि = एतान् these हन्तुम्- killing इच्छामि - I desire, घ्नतोऽपि - घ्नतः, killed, अपि even मधुसूदन - O, Krishna (One who killed the demon Madhu), अपि even त्रैलोक्यराज्यस्य - rule over the three worlds हेतोः -purpose किं what नु महीकृते - for the sake of the earth

These I do not wish to kill, though they kill me, O Krishna, even if for ruling the three worlds, let alone for the purpose of killing them for the sake of the earth!

Commentary 1.35

Lord Krishna is known by many names (refer Vishnu Sahasranamam for thousand names). In this verse, Arjuna addresses Krishna as Madhusudana – the killer of the demon Madhu. In Sanskrit, names are often derived from lineage (like Janaki, daughter of King Janaka), qualities/features or achievements like Madhusudana. He expresses the dejection in his mind and does not want to fight this war even if he eventually gets to rule the three worlds let alone the earth. त्रैलोक्यराज्यस्य -The three worlds refer to the earth, the heavens and the intermediate world. In short, Arjuna declines to fight against the Kauravas.

Verse 1.36

निहत्य धार्तराष्ट्रान्नः का प्रीतिः स्याज्जनार्दन ।

पापमेवाश्रयेदस्मान्हत्वैतानाततायिनः ॥ १-३६॥

Nihatya dhaartaraashtraan nah kaa preetih syaaj janaardana;
Paapam evaashrayed asmaan hatwaitaan aatataayinah 1.36

Explanation to Verse 1.36

निहत्य = नि + हन्(R- to kill) – By killing धार्तराष्ट्रान्: - sons of Dhritarashtra (P, M), का -what प्रीतिः - pleasure (F) स्याज्जनार्दन -=स्यात् (अस् **R 'to be**) + जनार्दन - जनस्य अर्दनम् - one, who torments (evil) people, पापमेवाश्रयेदस्मान्हत्वैतानाततायिनः - long sentence with sandhi to be split as: पापम् - sin (S, N) एव - only, आश्रयेत् -accrue अस्मात्, ours हत्वा - (हन् **R)** – by killing एतान् आततायिनः - these felons

By killing these sons of Dhritarashtra, what pleasure can be ours, O Janardana? Only sin will accrue by killing these felons.

Commentary 1.36

One more name for Lord Krishna – Janardhana meaning one who is worshipped by people. Arjuna continues to reason his thinking. He asks Krishna what pleasure the Pandavas will get by killing the felons (sons of Dhritarashtra). The word 'aatataayinah' means those who commit serious crimes - felons or criminals. This word is used here because the Kauravas were really criminals as they tried to kill the Pandavas through various means of treachery.

Arjuna's vision is confusing as he says that only sins will accrue to the Pandavas by killing these criminals. Arjuna finds ways to wriggle out of his duty to fight, even though he, as a Kashatriya is expected to fight to uphold dharma. He displays a lack of discrimination, a sense of proper judgement. Such a weakness or mental conflict is termed *Sokah.* Don't we also encounter such situations where judgement gets clouded?

Verse 1.37

तस्मान्नार्हा वयं हन्तुं धार्तराष्ट्रान्स्वबान्धवान् ।

स्वजनं हि कथं हत्वा सुखिनः स्याम माधव ॥ १-३७॥

Tasmaan naarhaa vayam hantum dhaartaraashtraan swabaandhavaan;

Swajanam hi katham hatwaa sukhinah syaama maadhava 1-37

Explanation to Verse 1.37

तस्मान्नार्हा=- तस्मात् +न +अर्हा: -Therefore, not deserving वयं - we हन्तुं - killing धार्तराष्ट्रान्स्वबान्धवान् - the sons of Dhritarashtra (who are) our own kith and kin स्वजनं - our own relatives हि - only कथं -how हत्वा by killing them सुखिनः happy स्याम माधव - O Madhava?

Therefore, we should not kill the sons of Dhritarashtra, our relatives; for, how can we be happy by killing our own people, O Madhava (Krishna)?

Commentary 1.37

Addressing Krishna as Madhava, Arjuna advances his argument further. He concludes with the word 'Tasmaat' meaning therefore, we should not kill the sons of Dhritarashtra. He questions Krishna by asking 'what happiness can we get by killing our own people (swajanam).?

Verse 1.38

यद्यप्येते न पश्यन्ति लोभोपहतचेतसः ।

कुलक्षयकृतं दोषं मित्रद्रोहे च पातकम् ॥ १-३८॥

Yadyapyete na pashyanti lobhopahatachetasah;

Kulakshayakritam dosham mitradrohe cha paatakam. 1-38

Explanation to Verse 1.38

यद्यप्येते -= यद्यपि - यदि + अपि - even if न पश्यन्ति not see लोभोपहतचेतसः= लोभो (**R** लुभ् - entice, लोभ - greed,) + पहत -overpowered, caught + चेतसः mind, intellect कुलक्षयकृतं - causing destruction of families दोषं - evil मित्रद्रोहे - hostility or hurt to friends च -and पातकम् - sin

Though they (Kauravas), with intelligence overpowered by greed, see no evil in the destruction of families, and no sin in hostility to friends.

Commentary 1.38

This verse indicates that Arjuna seems clear on the reason for this war. He thinks that his enemies have come to fight because their intelligence is too cloudy and hence, they are too greedy. Because of their confusion, they have come to this battlefield. They do not realize the consequences of war, the destruction to families and the sins arising from hostility to friends.

Verse 1.39

कथं न ज्ञेयमस्माभिः पापादस्मान्निवर्तितुम् ।

कुलक्षयकृतं दोषं प्रपश्यद्भिर्जनार्दन ॥ १-३९॥

Katham na jneyam asmaabhih paapaad asmaan nivartitum;

Kulakshayakritam dosham prapashyadbhir janaardana 1-39

Explanation to Verse 1.39

कथं न - Why not, ज्ञेयम् - (R "ज्ञा" to know) what is known इदम् - this, निवर्तितुम् - (नि + वृत् - withdraw) stay away प्रपश्यद्भि: -(प्र + दृश्) – see clearly, कुलक्षयकृतं दोषं - evil in destroying the family

Why should not we, who clearly see evil in the destruction of a family, stay away from this sin, O Janardana (Krishna)

Commentary 1.39

After blaming the Kauravas for their inferior intelligence and greed, Arjuna addresses Krishna as *Janaradhana* and asks, "Why can't we think of withdrawing from such sinful actions, because we can see the evil in this war?" Arjuna is seeking the support of Krishna to his reasoning. (Many of us seek the support of others to our thinking.)

Verse 1.40

कुलक्षये प्रणश्यन्ति कुलधर्माः सनातनाः ।
धर्मे नष्टे कुलं कृत्स्नमधर्मोऽभिभवत्युत ॥ १-४० ॥

Kulakshaye pranashyanti kuladharmaah sanaatanaah;
Dharme nashte kulam kritsnam adharmo'bhibhavatyuta.

Explanation to Verse 1.40

कुलक्षये = कुलस्य क्षयः - कुल - family, lineage + क्षय destruction कुलधर्माः - कुलस्य धर्मः - धर्मः rituals and traditions प्रणश्यन्ति = प्र + नश् - to perish; सनातनाः eternal, immemorial धर्मे + नष्टे - rituals + destroy, कृत्स्नम् – entire अधर्मः non-righteousness, अभिभवति -अभि + भू - to prevail

In the destruction of a family, the immemorial religious rites of the family perish; following the destruction of rituals, impiety overcomes the whole family.

Commentary 1.40

Arjuna explains briefly the consequences of a war. With the destruction of families in the war, family traditions also perish. When longstanding family traditions are lost, adharma (unrighteousness) takes over.

Verse 1.41

अधर्माभिभवात्कृष्ण प्रदुष्यन्ति कुलस्त्रियः ।

स्त्रीषु दुष्टासु वार्ष्णेय जायते वर्णसङ्करः ॥ १-४१ ॥

Adharmaabhibhavaat krishna pradushyanti kulastriyah;

Streeshu dushtaasu vaarshneya jaayate varnasankarah 1-41

Explanation to Verse 1.41

अधर्माभिभवात् - अधर्म + अभिभवः non-righteousness prevails, कृष्ण - O' Krishna, प्रदुष्यन्ति = प्र + दुष् R -to become corrupted, कुलस्त्रियः women of the family, वार्ष्णेय - descendant of वृष्णी, स्त्रीषु- women दुष्टासु -mailgned, जायते - to become (from जन् R to be born) वर्णसङ्करः intermingling and confusion of Varnas (classes of people)

By prevalence of non-righteousness, O Krishna, the women of the family become corrupt and, women becoming corrupted, O Varshneya (descendant of Vrishni), leads to intermingling of classes of people!

Commentary 1.41

Arjuna continues to foresee the impact of war. When traditions are lost and dharma takes over the surviving families, women of families get corrupted. The result of such corruption is intermixture of castes.

Verse 1.42

सङ्करो नरकायैव कुलघ्नानां कुलस्य च ।

पतन्ति पितरो ह्येषां लुप्तपिण्डोदककक्रियाः ॥ १-४२ ॥

Sankaro narakaayaiva kulaghnaanaam kulasya cha;

Patanti pitaro Hesham luptapindodakakriyaah 1-42

Explanation to Verse 1.42

सङ्करो - arising from the confusion (of varnas), कुलघ्नानां - कुलघ्न - that which causes destruction of family कुलस्य - of the family, च and, नरकाय hell, एव only, एषाम् -this पितर: - fore-fathers (P), पतन्ति - fall down, हि - certainly, लुप्ता - (from R लुप् to loose) be lost/deprived पिण्डोदकक्रिया: =पिण्डं च उदकम् च क्रिया: Rice balls + water + rites

Confusion of castes leads the killers of the family to hell, for their forefathers fall, deprived of the offerings of rice-ball and water

Commentary 1.42

The Vedas prescribe a classification of people and certain duties for each class of people. When people of different classifications (varnas) marry, there is a likelihood of confusion of which tradition or duties to follow. Because of the intermixture, rituals like annual ceremonies (shraddams) to ancestors may not be performed.

Verse 1.43

दोषैरेतै: कुलघ्नानां वर्णसङ्करकारकै: ।

उत्साद्यन्ते जातिधर्मा: कुलधर्माश्च शाश्वता: ॥ १-४३ ॥

Doshair etaih kulaghnaanaam varnasankarakaarakaih;

Utsaadyante jaatidharmaah kuladharmaashcha shaashwataah 1-43

Explanation to Verse 1.43

दोषै: - by evil deeds, एतै: (P) these, कुलघ्नानां - destroyers of the family, वर्णसङ्करकारकै: that caused confusion of castes शाश्वता: eternal, permanent, जातिधर्मा: religious rites of a caste, उत्साद्यन्ते =

(उत् + सद् - to uproot, destroy) get destroyed

By these evil deeds of the destroyers of the family, which cause confusion of castes, the eternal religious rites of the caste and the family are destroyed

Commentary 1.43

Arising from the bad deeds of the destroyers of families, the intermixture of castes results in the loss of perpetual family-traditions.

Verse 1.44

उत्सन्नकुलधर्माणां मनुष्याणां जनार्दन ।
नरके नियतं वासो भवतीत्यनुशुश्रुम ॥ १-४४॥

Utsannakuladharmaanaam manushyaanaam janaardana;
Narake'niyatam vaaso bhavateetyanushushruma 1-44

Explanation to Verse 1.44

जनार्दन, Janardhana – O Krishna, उत्सन्नकुलधर्माणाम् = उत्सन्नाः कुलधर्माः यस्य सः one who has suffered the uprooting of family rituals, मनुष्याणाम् - for men अनियतम् - न नियतं, indefinite वास: to live, भवतीत्यनुशुश्रुम -=भवति + इति + अनुशुश्रुम -(अनु+श्रु - to hear) - be   + is + have heard

We have heard, O Janardana, that the dwelling for an unknown period in hell is inevitable for those men in whose families the religious practices have been destroyed!

Commentary 1.44

Arjuna tells Krishna (O' Janardhana) - we have heard that hell is the lasting abode for the men whose family traditions and religious practices are broken.

Verse 1.45

अहो बत महत्पापं कर्तुं व्यवसिता वयम् ।

यद्राज्यसुखलोभेन हन्तुं स्वजनमुद्यताः ॥ १-४५॥

Aho bata mahat paapam kartum vyavasitaa vayam;

Yadraajya sukhalobhena hantum swajanam udyataah 1-45

Explanation to Verse 1.45

अहो बत - Oh God, Alas महत् पापं - great sin कर्तुं - **doing** व्यवसिता: are engaged वयम् - we राज्यसुख - pleasures of a kingdom लोभेन - through greed, हन्तुं -to kill स्वजनम् - own kith and kin उद्यता: prepared

Alas! We are involved in a great sin in that we are prepared to kill our own kinsmen through greed for the pleasures of a kingdom.

Commentary 1.45

Arjuna laments again – Alas! Driven by the greed of enjoying the pleasures of a kingdom, we are prepared to kill our people and commit the sinful action.

Verse 1.46

यदि मामप्रतीकारमशस्त्रं शस्त्रपाणयः ।

धार्तराष्ट्रा रणे हन्युस्तन्मे क्षेमतरं भवेत् ॥ १-४६॥

Yadi maam aprateekaaram ashastram shastrapaanayah;

Dhaartaraashtraa rane hanyus tanme kshemataram bhavet. 1-46

Explanation to Verse 1.46

यदि - if (C) मामप्रतीकारमशस्त्रं = माम् + अप्रतीकारम् + अशस्त्रम् = I + unresisting + unarmed धार्तराष्ट्रा: - sons of Dhritarashtra, शस्त्रपाणयः - with arms in hand रणे - in battle, हन्युस्तन्मे = हन्युः + तत् + मे - kill + that + me क्षेमतरं - better भवेत् to become

If the sons of Dhritarashtra, with weapons in hand, should kill me in battle, unresisting and unarmed, that would be better for me

Commentary 1.46

Closing his arguments, Arjuna tells Krishna that even if the sons of Dhritarashtra armed with weapons kills him, unarmed and unresisting, that would be better for him. The despondency of Arjuna is at its peak.

Verse 1. 47 Sanjaya Speaks

सञ्जय उवाच ।

एवमुक्त्वार्जुनः सङ्ख्ये रथोपस्थ उपाविशत् ।

विसृज्य सशरं चापं शोकसंविग्नमानसः ॥ १-४७ ॥

Sanjaya Uvaacha:

Evamuktwaa'rjunah sankhye rathopastha upaavishat;

Visrijya sasharam chaapam shokasamvignamaanasah 1-47

Explanation to Verse 1.47

सञ्जयः उवाच - Sanjaya said: एवम् उक्त्वा - thus spoken, अर्जुनः Arjuna संख्ये - in the battlefield, रथोपस्थः = रथं + उपस्थः - Chariot seat उपाविशत् - sat down विसृज्य - discarding सशरं =सह + शरम् - with arrow शोकसंविग्नमानसः = शोकेन संविग्नं मानसः - mind afflicted with sorrow

Sanjaya said:

Having thus spoken in the midst of the battlefield, Arjuna, casting away his bow and arrow, sat down on the seat of the chariot with his mind overwhelmed with sorrow.

Commentary 1.47

This is the concluding verse of Chapter 1 called Arjuna Vishada Yoga (The despondency of Arjuna). In this verse, Sanjaya tells Dhritarashtra:

"After having spoken thus in the battlefield, the grief-stricken Arjuna, sat down on the seat of the chariot, abandoning the bow and arrows."

3.1 End of Chapter 1 on Vishadayoga

ॐ तत्सदिति श्रीमद्भगवद्गीतासूपनिषत्सु

ब्रह्मविद्यायां योगशास्त्रे श्रीकृष्णार्जुनसंवादे

अर्जुनविषादयोगो नाम प्रथमोऽध्यायः ॥ १ ॥

Hari Om Tat Sat Iti Srimad Bhagavadgeetaasoopanishatsu Brahmavidyaayaam Yogashaastre Sri Krishnaarjunasamvaade Arjunavishaadayogo Naama Prathamo'dhyaayah. 1

3.2 Chapter 1 Conclusion

Thus, in the Upanishads of the glorious Bhagavad Gita, the science of the Eternal, the scripture of Yoga, the dialogue between Sri Krishna and Arjuna, ends the first discourse entitled: Arjuna Vishaada Yogah ("The Yoga of the Despondency of Arjuna")

Sri Haraye Namah! Sri Haraye Namah! Sri Haraye Namah!

3.3 Summary of Chapter 1

Introduction of the key soldiers in the two armies (Kauravas and Pandavas) assembled at Kurukshetra.

Arjuna requested Krishna to place his chariot between them so that he might survey his opponents.

On seeing his preceptors, relatives and friends, Arjuna was bewildered.

Confusion reigned in Arjuna's mind. Should he participate in this terrible carnage? Was it proper to destroy one's relatives for the sake of a kingdom and some pleasures?

Like a weakling, Arjuna does not want to fight and lays down his arms.

4 Srimad Bhagavad Gita – Chapter 2- Sankhya Yoga

द्वितीयोऽध्यायः। साङ्ख्ययोगः

Sankhya Yogah - The Yoga of Knowledge

We start with introductory comments to help readers in better understanding of the contents of this important chapter. Throughout the first chapter, Krishna DOES NOT SAY A WORD. This contains a LESSON. One should fully listen to understand what the other person has in his mind. Most people often react immediately before listening fully what the other person has to say.

The second chapter of Gita is entitled "The Sankhya Yoga". This contains the essence of Bhagavad Gita. The second Chapter can be classified into 4 main topics as under:

1st Topic – Arjuna Charanagadhi – The Surrender of Arjuna (Verses 1 to 10).

2nd Topic – Gnana Yoga –The Yoga of Knowledge (Verses 11 to 38).

3rd Topic – Karma Yoga – The Yoga of Duty (Verses 39 to 53).

4th Topic – About Sthitaprajna, a person of steady mind (Verses 54 to 72).

Each topic conveys a message and some lessons. To begin with, let us see a summary of each topic:

1. Arjuna Charanagadhi

In the battlefield, Arjuna suffered from the problem of samsara - *rāgaḥ, śokaḥ and mohaḥ* (attachment, sorrow and conflict/delusion). Unable to solve this problem, he feels helpless and finally chooses to surrender to Lord Krishna who now assumes the role of Jagadguru. The lesson we learn from this topic is that Humility and Total surrender to a Guru are essential to find solutions.

2. Gnana Yoga or Sankhya Yoga

Krishna discusses the essential nature of every individual. What is *Atma (soul) or Jeeva Swaroopam?* Who am I in reality? He clarifies that people do not function only through physical body; when you wake up, you use this body, and when you go to sleep, you keep aside your physical body, even the mind is not operational during sleep; Atma itself is not the body, mind or sense organs. These are only the medium through which 'I 'the atma functions. Atma is different and is of the nature of consciousness principle.

Krishna adopts a multipronged approach to persuade Arjuna to fight. To begin with, Lord Krishna talks philosophy - about Atma and its eternal six distinctive qualities – *Nityah* (Eternal, Everlasting), *Satyah* (Truth), *Sarvagatah* (Omnipresent), *Aprameyah* (Subject, Experiencer), *Akartaa-abhoktaa;* (No action nor Fruits), *Nirvikaarah* (Free from changes).

3. Karma Yoga

The second approach adopted by Lord Krishna relates to the practice of Karma *Yoga*, an option, that is considered as failproof. It is about performing proper rightful action as one's own duty. It is about enjoying what you do, following dharma (righteousness) as your duty, with proper attitude. Such actions are considered as offerings to the Lord and the consequent results as prasada, as the gift of the Lord. THE LESSON conveyed is - *Do your duty and do not expect fruits as you wish.*

4. About Sthitaprajnah – A person of steady mind

Sthitaprajnah means not only a person of intellectual knowledge but emotional strength to face life.

In this topic, Lord Krishna discusses the traits of Sthitaprajnah and how to acquire them. He mentions some of the important traits like: Freedom from binding desires, Samatvam or equanimity of mind Freedom from fear and turbulences caused by anger, jealousy, greed and others.

Not only Lord Krishna mentions the desirable qualities of a *Sthithaprajnah*, He also suggests ways to acquire such qualities. He tells Arjuna about the various methods including *Indriya Nigrahah -* Control of Senses, *Mano Nigrahah* – Discipline of Thoughts, and others.

Verse 2-1

सञ्जय उवाच ।

तं तथा कृपयाविष्टमश्रुपूर्णाकुलेक्षणम् ।

विषीदन्तमिदं वाक्यमुवाच मधुसूदनः ॥ २-१ ॥

Sanjaya Uvaacha:

Tam tathaa kripayaavishtam ashrupoornaakulekshanam;

Visheedantam idam vaakyam uvaacha madhusoodanah. 2-1

Explanation to Verse 2-1

सञ्जय उवाच - Sanjaya said, तं - him (Arjuna) तथा - thus, कृपया - from कृपा - compassion/pity, आविष्ट- overcome, अश्रुपूर्णाकुलम् = अश्रु +पूर्ण + आकुलं - eyes filled with tear, ईक्षणम् - ईक्ष to see (S) विषीदन्तम् - to grieve, मधुसूदनः

= मधु + सूदनः - Madhu + who killed (S) – name for Krishna, इदम् - this, वाक्यमुवाच - spoke

Sanjaya said:

To him who was thus overcome with pity and who was despondent, with eyes full of tears and agitated, Krishna or Madhusudana (the destroyer of Madhu), spoke these words. 2-1

Commentary 2-1

In this verse, Sanjaya explains what happened at the battlefield following Arjuna's monologue.

Sanjaya says: "Looking at Arjuna's eyes filled with tears due to intense attachment, Krishna spoke these words." Tears come when a person is in deep sorrow not knowing what to do. Arjuna is now in such a sorrowful condition.

Verse 2.2 Bhagavan Speaks

श्रीभगवानुवाच ।

कुतस्त्वा कश्मलमिदं विषमे समुपस्थितम् ।

अनार्यजुष्टमस्वर्ग्यमकीर्तिकरमर्जुन ॥ २-२॥

Sri Bhagavaan Uvaacha:

Kutastwaa kashmalam idam vishame samupasthitam;

Anaaryajushtam aswargyam akeertikaram arjuna.

Explanation to Verse 2-2

श्रीभगवानुवाच - श्रीभगवान् उवाच = श्रीः च भगः च अस्य - Bhagavan said, कुतस्त्वा = कुतः + त्वा, from where कश्मलमिदं - this विषमे improper समुपस्थितम् = सम् + उप + स्था - to arise, अनार्यजुष्टम् =अनार्य + जुष्टम् ignoble, disgraceful, अस्वर्ग्यम् - that would close the gates to heaven, अकीर्तिकरम् - which would make one unworthy, infamous, अर्जुन - O' Arjuna

Bhagavan, the Blessed Lord, said:

From where this perilous strait comes upon thee, this dejection which is unworthy of thee, disgraceful, and which will close the gates of heaven upon thee, O Arjuna 2-2

Commentary 2-2

Lord Krishna responds to Arjuna. He chides him. To begin with, the Lord uses harsh words that are likely to stir Arjuna into action. He says *'Kutaha idam kashmalam samupasthim'* – meaning from where did you get such impure thoughts? The impurity is in Arjuna's thinking arising out of disenchantment and frustration. While in exile, Arjuna (in disguise) had fought against the Kauravas. At that time, he did not have any regrets. So, Krishna seems to question – Hey Arjuna, you are a great warrior, how come that you are in such an emotional depression now? Such thoughts do not come to noble people. The word *'Arya'* indicates noble. Arya purusha refers to people of good character and integrity. Krishna points out to Arjuna that engaging in such negative thoughts will only lead to losing his fame and the path to heaven.

Verse 2-3

क्लैब्यं मा स्म गमः पार्थ नैतत्त्वय्युपपद्यते ।

क्षुद्रं हृदयदौर्बल्यं त्यक्त्वोत्तिष्ठ परन्तप ॥ २-३ ॥

Klaibyam maa sma gamah paartha naitat twayyupapadyate;
Kshudram hridaya daurbalyam tyaktwottishtha parantapa. 2-3

Explanation to Verse 2-3

क्लैब्यं - from क्लैब्य - impotence, unmanliness, cowardice मा – not स्म - to happen गमः to go पार्थ - son of Pritha (Arjuna) एतत् - this, त्वयि - युष्मद् pronoun of second person, उपपद्यते = उप + पद् does not befit, क्षुद्रं -

mean हृदयदौर्बल्यम् = हृदयस्य दौर्बल्यम् - weakness of the heart, त्यक्त्वोत्तिष्ठ =तत् + त्यक्त्वा + त्वम् - this + discard + you उत्तिष्ठ - get up, परन्तप = Paramtapa = para another, tapa to heat or inflame – scorcher of another (enemies).

Yield not to impotence, O Arjuna, son of Pritha! It does not befit you. Cast off this mean weakness of the heart. Stand up, O scorcher of foes! 2-3

Commentary 2-3

Paartha is another name of Arjuna. It means son of Pritha, another name of his mother Kunti. Lord Krishna tries to stimulate Arjuna by saying, "Oh Paartha, Get up! Don't be chicken-hearted and unmanly. You are a brave warrior and a scorcher of enemies (parantapah); it is not befitting your great status to throw down arms now." On one hand, Krishna chides Arjuna, and on the other he praises him. Isn't it a great strategy to motivate someone?

Verse 2-4

अर्जुन उवाच ।

कथं भीष्ममहं सङ्ख्ये द्रोणं च मधुसूदन ।

इषुभिः प्रतियोत्स्यामि पूजार्हावरिसूदन ॥ २-४॥

Arjuna Uvaacha:

Katham bheeshmamaham sankhye dronam cha madhusoodana;
Ishubhih pratiyotsyaami poojaarhaavarisoodana. 2-4

Explanation to Verse 2-4

अर्जुन उवाच । Arjuna said,

कथं - how भीष्ममहं - भीष्मम् + अहम् Bhisma, I सङ्ख्ये - in battle द्रोणं च and Drona मधुसूदन - O Madhusudana, (destroyer of enemies) इषुभिः with arrow प्रतियोत्स्यामि = प्रति + युध् - fight against, पूजाहार्वरिसूदन = पूजाहैः - पूजायै Worship अर्हः deserve, fit अरिणां (अरि -enemy) सूदनः to kill

Arjuna said:

How, O Madhusudana, shall I fight in battle with arrows against Bhisma and Drona, who are fit to be worshipped, O destroyer of enemies? 2-4

Commentary 2-4

Some people respond to a stimulation immediately. For some others like Arjuna now, it takes time to act.

Arjuna is still in depression and laments again: Oh Krishna, how can I fight against respected people like Bhisma and Drona?

Verse 2-5

गुरूनहत्वा हि महानुभावान् श्रेयो भोक्तुं भैक्ष्यमपीह लोके ।

हत्वार्थकामांस्तु गुरूनिहैव भुञ्जीय भोगान् रुधिरप्रदिग्धान् ॥ २-५॥

Guroonhatwaa hi mahaanubhaavaan Shreyo bhoktum bhaikshyamapeeha loke;

Hatwaarthakaamaamstu guroonihaiva Bhunjeeya bhogaan rudhirapradigdhaan. 2-5

Explanation to Verse 2-5

गुरूनहत्वा = गुरून् + अहत्वा (हन्-R) –The Gurus + not slaying (instead of) हि indeed महानुभावान् -most noble, श्रेयो - better भोक्तुं - (भुज् R) to eat, भैक्ष्यमपीह = भैक्ष्यम +अपी +इह - alms + even + here in this लोके - world हत्वार्थकामांस्तु गुरूनिहैव = हत्वा having killed अर्थकामान्- wealth and desires, तु indeed, गुरून् इह एव - Gurus here also; भुञ्जीय - enjoy भोगान् - pleasures रुधिर - blood प्रदिग्धान् - (प्र + दिह्) - stained, smeared

Better it is, indeed, in this world to accept alms than to slay the most noble teachers. But if I kill them, even in this world all my enjoyments of wealth and desires will be stained with (their) blood. 2-5

Commentary 2-5

Arjuna knows that he has a problem but continues to justify his thoughts by thinking of other options. The word 'bhikṣa' is singular and refers to alms collected from a donor. Bhaikshyam is plural and means alms collected from several donors. Arjuna feels that it is better to live on such alms collected from many people rather than killing his Gurus and live on blood-stained wealth and pleasures. The guilt feeling of Arjuna is clearly expressed in this verse. He does not realize that Bhiksha is permitted only for some categories of people like brahmacharis (bachelors) and sanyaasis (saints). Arjuna is IGNORANT.

Verse 2-6

न चैतद्विद्मः कतरन्नो गरीयो यद्वा जयेम यदि वा नो जयेयुः ।

यानेव हत्वा न जिजीविषामस्- तेऽवस्थिताः प्रमुखे धार्तराष्ट्राः ॥ २-६ ॥

Na chaitad vidmah kataran no gareeyo Yadwaa jayema yadi vaa no jayeyuh;

Yaan eva hatwaa na jijeevishaamas Te'vasthitaah pramukhe dhaartaraashtraah. 2-6

Explanation to Verse 2-6

न -not चैतद्विद्मः = च and एतत् this विद्मः we know - कतरन्नो कतरत् which नः for us गरीयो - better, यद्वा - यदि that वा or जयेम - we should conquer यदि if, वा or नो us जयेयुः they should conquer यानेव - whom, even हत्वा having killed न not जिजीविषामस्- we wish to live तेऽवस्थिताः = ते - those अवस्थिताः (अव + स्था) – are standing प्रमुखे - facing धार्तराष्ट्राः- sons of Dhritarashtra

I can hardly tell which will be better: that we should conquer them, or they should conquer us. Even the sons of Dhritarashtra, after slaying whom we do not wish to live, stand facing us. 2-6

Commentary 2-6

Seeing his own cousins assembled to fight against him, Arjuna is in conflict in his own mind. To fight or not to fight is the question. The very first words of this verse are "na chaitadvidmaha" meaning 'we do not know.' Arjuna admits ignorance of not knowing who will win the war. By killng the Kauravas, Arjuna is not sure if the victory will make the Panadavas live happily. Arjuna is clearly in two minds and is unable to decide which way to go. Do we not face such situation in our own lives? Many people are in 'two minds' – whether to perform a task or not? How to decide? Gita shows a way.

Verse 2-7

कार्पण्यदोषोपहतस्वभावः पृच्छामि त्वां धर्मसम्मूढचेताः ।

यच्छ्रेयः स्यान्निश्चितं ब्रूहि तन्म शिष्यस्तेऽहं शाधि मां त्वां प्रपन्नम् ॥ २-७॥

Kaarpanyadoshopahataswabhaavah Pricchaami twaam dharmasammoodha chetaah;

Yacchreyah syaan nishchitam broohi tanme Shishyaste'ham shaadhi maam twaam prapannam. 2-7

Explanation to Verse 2-7

कार्पण्यदोषोपहतस्वभावः = कार्पण्यम् -miserliness, एव दोषः-limitation, उपहतः -overpowered स्वभावः -one's nature- यस्य -for whom, one who is overcome by faint-heartedness, or cowardice; पृच्छामि —I am asking; त्वाम्—to you; धर्मसम्मूढचेताः = धर्म-duty, सम्मूढ -confused, चेतः -mind, यस्य -for whom, यच्छ्रेयः = यत् —what; श्रेयः—best; स्यान्निश्चितं= स्यात् —may be; निश्चितम्—decisively; ब्रूहि-tell; तन्मे =

तत् -that मे —to me; शष्यिस्तेऽहं= शष्यि: —disciple; ते—your; अहम् —I; शाधि—**please instruct**;मां—me त्वां -unto you; प्रपन्ननम्—surrendered

Commentary 2-7

This is an important verse signalling Arjuna's confession and surrender to the Lord. Indicating his confusion and inability to decide what is right (dharmic), Arjuna seeks Krishna's help to guide him. He says, *'Aham Te Shishyah, Shaadi maam'* - I am your disciple, teach me. Having discovered the problem, and the helplessness in solving it, complete surrender to the Lord *('charanagathi'* as it is called) is indicated here to address one's most difficult problems.

Lesson: Knowledge is of two kinds. One that you know; the other that you know where to get it from. So, when you are unable to solve a problem, it is better to ask some one (usually a Guru) who can solve it for you.

Verse 2-8

न हि प्रपश्यामि ममापनुद्याद् यच्छोकमुच्छोषणमिन्द्रियाणाम् ।

अवाप्य भूमावसपत्नमृद्धं राज्यं सुराणामपि चाधिपत्यम् ॥ २-८॥

Na hi prapashyaami mamaapanudyaad Yacchokam ucchoshanam indriyaanaam;

Avaapya bhoomaavasapatnam riddham Raajyam suraanaam api chaadhipatyam. 2-8

Explanation to Verse 2-8

न हि प्रपश्यामि - I do not see. मम अपनुद्यात् = अपनुद्यात् -अप + नुद् **(R)**, to drive away, remove; यत् शोकम् - This grief, sorrow; उत्-शोषणम् = उत् + शुष्- become dry; इन्द्रियाणाम् - senses, body organs अवाप्य = अव + आप् - to attain; भूमावसपत्नमृद्धं =भूमौ - on earth, अ-सपत्नम् - without an enemy, ऋद्धं

- ऋध् **R** - to prosper; राज्यम् - kingdom (from R राज् - to rule, to be eminent सुराणाम् - Gods (Devas- from सुर R), अपि च also, and C आधिपत्यम् - Lordship (अधि + पति - Lord or Master)

I do not see that it would remove this sorrow that burns up my senses even if I should attain prosperity and unrivalled dominion on earth or lordship over the gods. 2-8

Commentary 2-8

Arjuna expresses again his anguish. He is unable to visualize anything that can clear his sorrow that weakens all his sense organs. He is not sure that even after winning a prosperous kingdom upon earth and getting the kingship over the gods whether his sorrow will get over.

Verse 2-9

सञ्जय उवाच ।

एवमुक्त्वा हृषीकेशं गुडाकेशः परन्तप ।

न योत्स्य इति गोविन्दमुक्त्वा तूष्णीं बभूव ह ॥ २-९॥

Sanjaya Uvaacha:

Evam uktwaa hrisheekesham gudaakeshah parantapah;

Na yotsya iti govindam uktwaa tooshneem babhoova ha.

Explanation to Verse 2-9

सञ्जय उवाच - **Sanjaya said:**

एवमुक्त्वा - एवम् उक्त्वा - Having spoken thus; हृषीकेशं to Hrishikesa (Krishna, Lord of the senses); गुडाकेशः - गुडाकायाः ईशः - One who has overcome sleep, Arjuna; परन्तप - परम् + तप् - others + heat - the scorcher of enemies, न योत्स्य (from R युध्)- I will not fight, इति said so गोविन्दमुक्त्वा to Govinda तूष्णीं - silent बभूव **from** the R भू - to become, ह certainly

Having spoken thus to Hrishikesa (Lord of the senses), Arjuna (the conqueror of sleep), the destroyer of foes, said to Krishna: "I will not fight," and became silent. 2-9

Commentary 2-9

Sanjaya is back with his commentary on the battlefield situation. He tells Dhritarashtra that Arjuna, the scorcher of enemies, spoke these words, declined to fight and became quiet.

Verse 2-10

तमुवाच हृषीकेशः प्रहसन्निव भारत ।

सेनयोरुभयोर्मध्ये विषीदन्तमिदं वचः ॥ २-१० ॥

Tam uvaacha hrisheekeshah prahasanniva bhaarata;
Senayor ubhayor madhye visheedantam idam vachah.

Explanation to Verse 2-10

तमुवाच - तम् + उवाच - spoke these, हृषीकेशः Rishikesha: -Krishna प्रहसन्निव = प्रहसन् (Root हस to laugh) + इव - smilingly + as if; भारत , O Bharata (भरतस्य वंशजः भारतः) Born in the lineage of renowned King Bharat; सेनयोरुभयोर्मध्ये - In the midst of two armies; विषीदन्तमिदं = विषीदन्तम् + इदम् - (वि + सद् to grieve), sorrowful, despondent वचः words

To him who was despondent in the midst of the two armies, Sri Krishna, as if smiling, O Bharata, spoke these words! 2-10

Commentary 2-10

In this verse Sanjaya addresses Dhritarashtra as *'Bharata' – one who belongs to the lineage of King Bharat.* Sanjaya informs him that Lord Krishna smilingly spoke the following words to the grieving Arjuna who was standing between the two armies.

Verse 2-11

श्रीभगवानुवाच ।

अशोच्यानन्वशोचस्त्वं प्रज्ञावादांश्च भाषसे ।

गतासूनगतासूंश्च नानुशोचन्ति पण्डिताः ॥ २-११ ॥

Let' s Split the Sandhis in this verse –

अशोच्यान् अन्वशोच: त्वम् प्रज्ञावादान् च भाषसे ।

गतासून् अगतासून् च न अनुशोचन्ति पण्डिताः

Sri Bhagavaan Uvaacha:

Ashochyaan anvashocha stwam prajnaavaadaam cha bhaashase;

Gataasoon agataasoomshcha naanu shochanti panditaah 2-11

Explanation to Verse 2-11

अशोच्यान् - (from R शुच् to grieve, mourn) - not worthy of grieving; अन्वशोच: = अनु + शुच् - you grieve, त्वम् - you, thee प्रज्ञावादान् = (प्र + ज्ञा -to possess knowledge) intelligent; वादान् - (Root वद् -to talk) argument; च -and, भाषसे - speak, गतासून् = (Root गम् to go) gone or dead[अगतासून् - not dead , meaning living च - and , न - do not[अनुशोचन्ति – grieve; पण्डिताः - the wise, the learned

Sri Bhagavan (the Blessed Lord) said:

You grieved for those that are not worthy to be grieved for, and yet you speak learned words. The wise grieve neither for the living nor for the dead. 2-11

Commentary 2-11

See how beautifully the words are joined together. In Sanskrit, words start from roots and sprout like a lovely plant! Beginning from this verse, Lord Krishna starts His most important teachings (*upadesam*). It is a very important verse as it is forming the core of Gita, signaling the message that ignorance is the basic cause of all human problems. Lord Krishna tells Arjuna that he is grieving for people who should not be grieved while thinking he is wise. Panditaha means wise people. Krishna says *'pandithah na anusochanti'* - wise people do not grieve either for the dead or for the living.

Verse 2-12

न त्वेवाहं जातु नासं न त्वं नेमे जनाधिपाः ।

न चैव न भविष्यामः सर्वे वयमतः परम् ॥ २-१२॥

Na twevaaham jaatu naasam na twam neme janaadhipaah;
Na chaiva na bhavishyaamah sarve vayam atah param. 2-12

Explanation to Verse 2-12

न त्वेवाहं = न never+ तु but +एव indeed+अहं I; जातु- anytime; नासं = न was not आसं - (Root अस्- to be) exist; न त्वं नेमे = न not + त्वम् you, न इमे - nor these; जनाधिपाः - जनानां अधिपः जनाधिपः one who leads people, the rulers; न चैव - न च एव - never also certainly; भविष्यामः -shall exist; सर्वे वयमतः परम् = सर्वे वयम् all of us + अतः परम् hereafter.

Never was there any time that I did not exist, nor you nor these rulers of men, nor verily shall we ever cease to be hereafter (in the future) 2-12

Commentary 2-12

There is deep philosophy in this verse. Lord Krishna gives an indication about the eternal 'Atma' or soul, being different from the physical body. The Atma is permanent though bodies appear and die. It existed before and will exist in the future also. This applies to all those present in the battlefield (and hence there is no need to grieve)

Verse 2-13

देहिनोऽस्मिन्यथा देहे कौमारं यौवनं जरा ।

तथा देहान्तरप्राप्तिर्धीरस्तत्र न मुह्यति ॥ २-१३॥

Dehino'smin yathaa dehe kaumaaram yauvanam jaraa;

Tathaa dehaantara praaptir dheeras tatra na muhyati. 2-13

Explanation to Verse 2-13

देहिनोऽस्मिन्यथा = देहिन: having a body, embodied (soul), अस्मिन् this, यथा - just as देहे body; कौमारं – childhood; यौवनं -youth; जरा -old age; तथा, likewise; देहान्तरप्राप्तिर्धीरस्तत्र= देहान्तर-अन्य: देह: देहान्तरम् - another body, प्राप्ति - प्राप्ति: - प्र + आप् - to get, obtain धीरस्तत्र - धीर: the bold, valiant + तत्र – thereat; न मुह्यति - does not grieve

Just as in this body the embodied (soul) passes into childhood, youth and old age, so also does the soul pass into another body; the bold man does not grieve thereat (at such a change)- 2-13

Commentary 2-13

Lord Krishna provides an analogy of a human body. Just as the body goes through different stages in life, starting as a child, progressing to youth and eventually old age, attaining different forms in life, the soul too attains (migrates) another body. Changes relate to only the physical body, but the Atma or Self does not change despite the migration. The wise people who know this do not worry about such transformation.

Verse 2-14

मात्रास्पर्शास्तु कौन्तेय शीतोष्णसुखदुःखदाः ।

आगमापायिनोऽनित्यास्तांस्तितिक्षस्व भारत ॥ २-१४॥

Split Sandhi

मात्रास्पर्शाः तु कौन्तेय शीत-ऊष्णसुखदुःखदाः
आगम-अपायिनः अनित्याः तान् तितिक्षस्व भारत

Maatraa sparshaastu kaunteya sheeto shnasukhaduhkhadaah;
Aagamaapaayinoanityaas taams titikshaswa bhaarata. 2-14

Explanation to Verse 2-14

मात्रास्पर्शाः = मात्रा material + स्पर्शः to touch - materialistic sensory perceptions; तु only; कौन्तेय - son of Kunti (Arjuna); शीत-ऊष्णसुखदुःखदाः = शीतम् - शीतः cold + ऊष्णम् -ऊष्ण: heat + सुखम् -सुखः happiness + दुःखम् -दुःख – sorrow; आगम-अपायिनः = आगमः To come, अपायः to go, harm; अनित्याः - not permanent; तान्- all of them; तितिक्षस्व - endure, tolerate; भारत, O Arjuna descendent of the Bharata dynasty

The sensory contacts with materialistic objects, O son of Kunti, that cause heat and cold, pleasure and pain, have a beginning and an end; they are impermanent; endure them bravely, O Arjuna! 2-14

Commentary 2-14

Addressing Arjuna as Kaunteya (son of Kunti), Krishna asks him to accept the fact that the feelings of heat and cold sensed by the senses are temporary, and he must bear them patiently. Resistance to such facts can only lead to sorrow. THE LESSON here is that one must learn to live with situations, show patience rather than resist them or run away.

Pain and pleasure are purely transitory. The quality of bearing them with endurance is called here as *'titiksa.'*

Verse 2-15

यं हि न व्यथयन्त्येते पुरुषं पुरुषर्षभ ।
समदुःखसुखं धीरं सोऽमृतत्वाय कल्पते ॥ २-१५॥

Yam hi na vyatha yantyete purusham purusha arshabha;
Samaduhkha sukham dheeram soAmritatwaaya kalpate. 2-15

Explanation to Verse 2-15

Split Sandhi

यं - one to whom, हि -certainly न - not ; व्यथयन्ति = (व्यथ् -pain) –is not disturbed एते all these; पुरुषं -to a man (person); पुरुषर्षभ - पुरुषेषु - among men, ऋषभः excellent; सम equanimity, even दुःखसुखं in happiness or sorrow; धीरं - bold, firm सोऽमृतत्वाय = सः - he अमृतत्वाय - immortality, eternal; कल्पते- eligible

O best among men (Arjuna), the firm man who is not disturbed by happiness or distress (who is cool!), and is steady in both situations is certainly eligible for immortality 2-15

Commentary 2-15

The person who is not impacted by pain or pleasures, who is balanced in both, is the one is suited to attain knowledge of the Self. Such a person is described here as *'Dheerah'* – an intelligent one with the power of discrimination. He is one who accepts what cannot be changed. He does not get angry, irritated or ruffled by events on which he has no control. Such a person enjoys a peace of mind. (See the beauty of rhyming Sanskrit words: *Veera Dheera Shoora* meaning valor, courage, and strength).

Verse 2-16

नासतो विद्यते भावो नाभावो विद्यते सतः ।
उभयोरपि दृष्टोऽन्तस्त्वनयोस्तत्त्वदर्शिभिः ॥ २-१६ ॥

Naasato vidyate bhaavo naabhaavo vidyate satah;
Ubhayorapi drishto'ntastwanayos tattwadarshibhih. 2-16

Explanation to Verse 2-16

नासतो = न never + असत: (न सत् इति असत्) – non-existent (सत् means what exists, truth, noble), विद्यते - there is भावो - (root verb भू to be), enduring नाभावो - न अभाव: never changing quality विद्यते -there is सत: - of the eternal उभयोरपि दृष्टोऽन्तस्त्वनयोस्तत्त्वदर्शिभि: - split sandhi as = उभयो: अपि दृष्ट: अन्त: तु अनयो: तत्त्व दर्शिभि: उभयो: -of the two अपि - verily दृष्ट:seen अन्त: -end तु -indeed अनयो: of them, तत्त्व of the truth दर्शिभि:- by the seers

The unreal (the material body) has no enduring quality; there is no change of the Real (soul); the truth about both has been seen by the the seers. 2-16

Commentary 2-16

Again, Lord Krishna talks philosophy, about the nature of Atma – the Self. He says that Atma is real while anaatma is unreal.

A popular example is that of a pot made from clay. When the clay is shaped into a pot, it gets the name of 'pot.' If we break the pot, the pot loses its name and existence. So, the pot had only a temporary existence borrowed from the clay. The clay existed even before the formation of the pot and continues to exist even after the pot is broken. Likewise, the Atma is permanent and real (like the clay) while the body, like a pot, is temporary that has borrowed the existence from the Atma. Atma is known as the 'Self' or pure consciousness. The wise seers understood the nature of Atma and anaatma. The Upanishads tell a lot about this reality.

Verse 2-17

अविनाशि तु तद्विद्धि येन सर्वमिदं ततम् ।

विनाशमव्ययस्यास्य न कश्चित्कर्तुमर्हति ॥ २-१७॥

Avinaashi tu tad viddhi yena sarvam idam tatam;

Vinaasham avyayasyaasya na kashchit kartum arhati. 2-17

Explanation to Verse 2-17

अविनाशि = न विनाशि इति अविनाशि – indestructible; तु –indeed, तद्विद्धि = तत् विद्धि – that know; येन सर्वमिदं ततम् - what has caused all this spread; विनाशमव्ययस्यास्य =विनाशम् अस्य = to destroy this, अव्ययस्य (from व्यय: =वि + अय् to deplete) = what is constant or eternal; न- not, कश्चित्कर्तुमर्हति = कश्चित् - कः + चित् none, nobody कर्तुं cause अर्हति –capable of

Know this "That" which has pervaded is indestructible. None is capable to cause the destruction of "That" - the Imperishable. 2-17

Commentary 2-17

Krishna says that the Atma is imperishable. None can destroy it. Atma is all-pervading like space.

Verse 2-18

अन्तवन्त इमे देहा नित्यस्योक्ताः शरीरिणः ।

अनाशिनोऽप्रमेयस्य तस्माद्युध्यस्व भारत ॥ २-१८॥

Antavanta ime dehaa nityasyoktaah shareerinah;
Anaashino'prameyasya tasmaad yudhyaswa bhaarata. 2-18

Explanation to Verse 2-18

अन्तवन्त = अन्तः अस्य अस्ति - One that has an end; इमे –this; देहा -body; नित्यस्योक्ताः = नित्यस्य –eternal + उक्ता: - spoken of. Said to be; शरीरिणः (assumes) the body; अनाशिनो = न नाशिन् – indestructible; ऽप्रमेयस्य- incomparable; तस्माद्युध्यस्व = तस्मात् (त्वम्) युध्यस्व – therefore you fight; भारत – O Bharata

These bodies of the embodied Self, which is eternal, indestructible and immeasurable, are said to have an end. Therefore, fight, O Arjuna! 2-18

Commentary 2-18

Since Atma is eternal and cannot be destroyed, and the bodies are perishable entities, Lord Krishna exhorts Arjuna to fight.

Verse 2-19

य एनं वेत्ति हन्तारं यश्चैनं मन्यते हतम् ।

उभौ तौ न विजानीतो नायं हन्ति न हन्यते ॥ २-१९॥

Ya enam vetti hantaaram yashchainam manyate hatam;

Ubhau tau na vijaaneeto naayam hanti na hanyate 2-19

Explanation to Verse 2-19

य एनं वेत्ति हन्तारं=- य: एनं हन्तारं (इति) वेत्ति - He, who understands him (it) as the killer; यश्चैनं मन्यते हतम् = य: च एनं हतम् मन्यते - and he who regards that it can be killed, उभौ तौ न विजानीतो- तौ उभौ न विजानीत: - both of them do not understand, नायं हन्ति न हन्यते - अयं न हन्ति न हन्यते - that it does not kill nor can it be killed

He, who takes the Self to be the slayer and he who thinks It is killed, neither of them knows; It slays not nor is It slain 2-19

Commentary 2-19

Elaborating further, Krishna says that the person who thinks Atma as a killer and another who thinks that Atma is killed, are both ignorant. Atma neither kills nor is killed. (Core of Hindu Philosophy)

Verse 2-20

न जायते म्रियते वा कदाचिन् –नायं भूत्वा भविता वा न भूयः ।

अजो नित्यः शाश्वतोऽयं पुराणो –न हन्यते हन्यमाने शरीरे ॥२-२०॥

Na jaayate mriyate vaa kadaachin Naayam bhootwaa
bhavitaa vaa na bhooyah;

Ajo nityah shaashwato'yam puraano Na hanyate
hanyamaane shareere. 2-20

Explanation to Verse 2-20

(अयं) - He (The Self or Atman) कदाचित् न – at any time जायते - born वा-
or म्रियते – dies अयं न – He (it) not भूत्वा – having come into existence
भविता – will come न not वा **or** भूयः come repeatedly. शरीरे हन्यमाने -
embodied in bodies that can be killed, अज: -unborn नित्यः:- eternal,
शाश्वत:- permanent, पुराण: ancient, अयं न हन्यते -He (it) cannot be killed
(*Note:* पुल्लिङ्गि प्रथमपुरुषे प्रथमा विभक्तिः एकवचनम्*)*

The Atman is neither born nor dies; It has been non-existent, nor does
it come into existence repeatedly. It is unborn, eternal, undecaying,
and ancient; It cannot be killed (even) when the body is killed. 2-20

Commentary 2-20

Yet another philosophy explained by Lord Krishna. The human body
goes through different phases – birth, existence, growth, changes in
forms, decay, and finally death. In contrast, Atma is never born nor
dies. It is free from decay and does not get old. It does not grow or
suffer changes

Verse 2-21

वेदाविनाशिनं नित्यम् य एनमजमव्ययम् ।
कथं स पुरुषः पार्थ कं घातयति हन्ति कम्।।२-२१।।

Vedaavinaashinam nityam ya enam ajam avyayam;

Katham sa purushah paartha kam ghaatayati hanti kam. 2-21

Explanation to Verse 2-21

वेद – knows अविनाशिनं- indestructible नित्यम् –eternal य –who एनम- this अजम – uborn अव्ययम् – immutable कथं – how स – he पुरुषः-man पार्थ – Partha कं -whom घातयति – causes to be killed हन्ति – kills कम् – whom

Whosoever knows Him to be indestructible, eternal, unborn and inexhaustible, how can that man slay, O Arjuna, or cause to be slain? 2-21

Commentary 2-21

Continuing, Lord Krishna tells, O Arjuna, the person who recognizes the Atma as imperishable, eternal, birthless, and changeless, how can he kill or cause another one to kill?

Verse 2-22

वासांसि जीर्णानि यथा विहाय । नवानि गृह्णाति नरोऽपराणि ।
तथा शरीराणि विहाय जीर्णा- न्यन्यानि संयाति नवानि देही ।।२-२२।।

Vaasaamsi jeernaani yathaa vihaaya Navaani grihnaati naro'paraani;

Tathaa shareeraani vihaaya jeernaa Nyanyaani samyaati navaani dehee 2-22

Explanation to Verse 2-22

वासांसि – garments जीर्णानि – worn out, यथा – just as विहाय - discard, cast off नवानि – new garment गृह्णाति – take, wear नरोऽपराणि - नर: - man अपराणि - **others** तथा – likewise शरीराणि – the bodies विहाय – discards जीर्णानि - old, worn-out, useless अन्यानि - others संयाति – enters नवानि – new देही - bodies

Just as a man casts off worn-out clothes and puts on new ones, so also the embodied Self casts off worn-out bodies and enters others that are new. 2-22

Commentary 2-22

This verse puts forth the theory of rebirth. Just as a person throws away the old clothes and wears new ones, so does the Atma casts away the old physical body and attains a new one. When someone dies, he discards his body. However, it is believed that the *'Sookshma Sareeram'* (the subtle body with the mind) continues. This is the core of **Jeevatma theory**.

Verse 2-23

नैनं छिन्दन्ति शस्त्राणि नैनं दहति पावकः ।
न चैनं क्लेदयन्त्यापो न शोषयति मारुतः ।।२-२३।।

Nainam cchindanti shastraani nainam dahati paavakah;

Na chainam kledayantyaapo na shoshayati maarutah. 2-23

Explanation to Verse 2-23

नैनं - न एनम् – never this (soul), छिन्दन्ति- cut to pieces शस्त्राणि – by weapons नैनं – nor this दहति – burns पावकः by fire; न चैनं – never also this क्लेदयन्त्यापो – gets wet by water न nor शोषयति – gets dry मारुतः by wind

Weapons cannot cut It (the Soul), fire does not burn It, water wets It not, nor is It get dried by wind. 2-23

Commentary 2-23

The human body gets impacted by the elements. Weapons (made from materials found from Mother Earth), Fire, Water, and Air can affect us. A sharp knife made of metal can cut us; likewise, fire can cause burn us and cause disasters; floods can cause havoc and drown us; air may get polluted and cause cold or diseases. Space or Akaasa is inert or actionless.

Atma is a unique entity that is not affected by any of these elements. Weapons do not cut it, fire does not burn it, water does not wet it and air too does not impact it.

Verse 2-24

अच्छेद्यः अयम् अदाह्यः अयम् अक्लेद्यः अशोष्यः एव च ।

नित्यः सर्वगतः स्थाणुः अचलः अयम् सनातनः ।।२-२४।।

Acchedyo'yam adaahyo'yam akledyo'shoshya eva cha;

Nityah sarvagatah sthaanur achalo'yam sanaatanah. 2-24

Explanation to Verse 2-24

अच्छेद्यः - cannot be cut or broken अयम् - this अदाह्यः - cannot be burnt अयम् – this soul अक्लेद्यः - cannot be wetted or dissolved अशोष्यः - cannot be dried एव – also च and नित्यः – everlasting सर्वगतः – all-pervading स्थाणुः - still (Note: There is a Shiva temple in Suchindram where Lord Shiva is called Sthanumurthy) अचलः - immoveable (For example, *Vindhyachal* is a mountain that is immoveable) अयम् - this सनातनः eternal

This Self cannot be cut, burnt, wetted nor dried up. It is eternal, all-pervading, stable, ancient and immovable.

Commentary 2-24

This verse repeats some of what is already said in verse 2.23. In addition, the nature of Atma is described as eternal, all-pervading, not bound by space limitations, still without showing any changes, motionless, and ancient. In short, the glory of Atma is briefly presented in this verse.

Verse 2-25

अव्यक्तोऽयमचिन्त्योऽयमविकार्योऽयमुच्यते ।

तस्मादेवं विदित्वेनं न त्वम् शोचितुमर्हसि ।।२-२५।।

Avyakto'yam achintyo'yam avikaaryo'yam uchyate;
Tasmaad evam viditwainam naanushochitum arhasi.

Explanation to Verse 2-25

Split first line into:

अव्यक्तः अयम् अचिन्त्यः अयम् अविकार्यः अयम् उच्यते;

अव्यक्त: = न व्यक्तः - not manifestedl अयम् - this अचिन्त्य: - न चिन्त्यः - beyond thoughts, inconceivable, अयम् अविकार्य: - न विकार्यः - unchangeable अयम् - It उच्यते - said to be;

Now the second line,

तस्मात् - therefore एवं - thus विदित्वा - having known एनं - this न - not त्वम् - you शोचितुम् - to grieve or lament अर्हसि - deserve

This (Self) is said to be unmanifested, unthinkable and unchangeable. Therefore, knowing 'This' to be such, thou should not grieve.

Commentary 2-25

Concluding the description of 'Atma,' Lord Krishna says that the Atma is unmanifested, imperceptible, unthinkable and unchangeable. Knowing such unique qualities of the 'Atma,' you should not grieve (as you are not killing the Atma).

Verse 2-26

अथ चैनं नित्यजातं नित्यं वा मन्यसे मृतम् ।
तथापि त्वं महाबाहो नैवं शोचितुमर्हसि ॥ २-२६ ॥

Atha chainam nityajaatam nityam vaa manyase mritam;
Tathaapi twam mahaabaaho naivam shochitum
arhasi 2-26

Explanation to Verse 2-26

अथ चैनं = अथ च एनं – Even if this (soul), नित्यजातं - forever-born, नित्यं वा - or forever, मन्यसे मृतम्- you think is dead, तथापि - even then, त्वं महाबाहो – you mighty-armed one (Arjuna,) नैवं = न एवम् – never about, शोचितुमर्हसि = शोचितुम् + अर्हसि – deserve to lament or grieve

Even if you think of It (soul) as being constantly born and dying, even then, O mighty armed, you should not lament! 2-26

Commentary 2-26

This verse provides a hypothetical statement from Lord Krishna. He addresses Arjuna as *'Mahaabaaho'* – O mighty armed and tells him that if you think that the Atma goes through births and deaths, even then you should feel sorry for it. There are different philosophies, and this verse is an example of how our ancient scriptures permit curiosity and questioning.

Verse 2-27

जातस्य हि ध्रुवो मृत्युर्ध्रुवं जन्म मृतस्य च ।
तस्मादपरिहार्येऽर्थे न त्वं शोचितुमर्हसि ॥ २-२७॥

Jaatasya hi dhruvo mrityur dhruvam janma mritasya cha;
Tasmaad aparihaarye'rthe na twam shochitum arhasi. 2-27

Explanation to Verse 2-27

जातस्य - जातस्य **from R** जन्- to be born हि - because ध्रुवो - certain, a fact मृत्युर्ध्रुवं – death is also sure जन्म मृतस्य च – birth and death तस्माद्- therefore अपरिहार्ये - unavoidable ऽर्थे – facts, in this matter न – not त्वं – you शोचितुमर्हसि - deserve to lament or grieve

Certain is death for the born and certain is birth for the dead; therefore, over the inevitable you should not grieve. 2-27

Commentary 2-27

Why should Arjuna not grieve? Lord Krishna explains the hypothesis in the earlier verse. Death is certain to anyone who is born. Going by the theory of rebirth, birth is also sure for one who is dead. This is a natural phenomenon. Therefore, you should not grieve over the inevitable. So, mourning over those who are dead is meaningless. THE LESSON here is to accept life as it is; birth and death are intrinsic part of it. You have little choice in this regard.

Verse 2-28

अव्यक्तादीनि भूतानि व्यक्तमध्यानि भारत ।

अव्यक्तनिधनान्येव तत्र का परिदेवना ॥ २-२८॥

Avyaktaadeeni bhootaani vyaktamadhyaani bhaarata;

Avyakta nidhanaanyeva tatra kaa paridevanaa. 2-28

Explanation to Verse 2-28

अव्यक्तादीनि = अव्यक्त-आदीनि –(वि + अञ्च् R, व्यक्त manifest) – unmanifested in the beginning, भूतानि – all that are created व्यक्तमध्यानि – manifested in the middle भारत – O Arjuna अव्यक्तनिधनान्येव = अव्यक्त + निधनानि + एव – unmanifested + when annihilated + like that तत्र – therefore, का – why परिदेवना – lament/grieve

All beings are unmanifested in the beginning, manifested in the middle state, O Arjuna, and unmanifested again in their end! What is there to grieve about? 2-28

Commentary 2-28

Life is something that is in between birth and death. It is transitory. Living beings have assumed physical forms in conformity with the law of nature. It is a conversion of the unmanifested into a manifested form. Therefore, lamenting over the death of individuals does not serve any useful purpose.

Verse 2-29

आश्चर्यवत्पश्यति कश्चिदेन-माश्चर्यवद्वदति तथैव चान्यः ।
आश्चर्यवच्चैनमन्यः श्रृणोति श्रुत्वाप्येनं वेद न चैव कश्चित् ॥ २-२९॥

Aashcharyavat pashyati kashchid enam Aashcharyavad vadati tathaiva chaanyah;

Aashcharyavacchainam anyah shrinoti Shrutwaapyenam veda na chaiva kashchit. 2-29

Explanation to Verse 2-29

आश्चर्यवत्पश्यति कश्चिदेनम= आश्चर्यवत् – as amazing, a wonder पश्यति – sees, कः-चित् – someone एनम् – this (soul), आश्चर्यवद्वदति तथैव चान्यः - तथा च (कश्चित्) अन्यः आश्चर्यवत् एव वदति - Also some other speaks of it as amazing आश्चर्यवच्चैनमन्यः श्रृणोति =अन्यः च एनम् आश्चर्यवत् श्रृणोति - Yet another hears of it as wondrous, श्रुत्वाप्येनं वेद न चैव कश्चित् = श्रुत्वा अपि च - Even after hearing of it कश्चित् एनं न वेद एव - No one understood it.

One sees This (the Self) as a wonder; another speaks of It as amazing; another hears of It as a wonder; yet, having heard, none understands It at all. 2-29

Commentary 2-29

Isn't this concept wonderful? It is difficult to classify or visualize the Atma as the 'Self.' One sees the Atma as a wonder. Another speaks about it as a wonderful thing. It is marvelleous. Yet another who hears about it does not know it at all. It is a wonder because the Atma happens to be one's own 'Self' and yet people look at it as an external object.

Verse 2-30

देही नित्यमवध्योऽयं देहे सर्वस्य भारत ।
तस्मात्सर्वाणि भूतानि न त्वं शोचितुमर्हसि ॥ २-३०॥

Dehee nityam avadhyo'yam dehe sarvasya bhaarata;
Tasmaat sarvaani bhootaani na twam shochitum arhasi. 2-30

Explanation to Verse 2- 30

देही – Inside or enshrined in the body, नित्यम् - permanent, अवध्य: - from R वध् to kill – cannot be killed, अयं this देहे – body, सर्वस्य – everyone, भारत – O, Arjuna (from the lineage of Bharata), तस्मात् – therefore, सर्वाणि भूतानि - all beings, न त्वम् शोचितुम् अर्हसि – you should not grieve

This, the Indweller in the body of everyone, is eternally indestructible, O Arjuna! Therefore, you should not grieve for all beings 2-30

Commentary 2-30

Addressing Arjuna as Bharata, Lord Krishna concludes his description of the Atma by saying that this Atma is present in everybody and is not destroyable. Therefore, O Arjuna, you should not grieve for anybody. Thus, Lord Krishna ends his philosophical approach to Arjuna's problem. In the next verse, He moves on to a pragmatic worldly approach.

Verse 2- 31

स्वधर्ममपि चावेक्ष्य न विकम्पितुमर्हसि ।
धर्म्याद्धि युद्धाच्छ्रेयोऽन्यत्क्षत्रियस्य न विद्यते ॥ २-३१॥

Swadharmam api chaavekshya na vikampitum arhasi;
Dharmyaaddhi yuddhaacchreyo'nyat kshatriyasya na vidyate. 2-31

Explanation to Verse 2-31

स्वधर्मम् - your own dharma (code of conduct), अपि - even च further अवेक्ष्य – considering, न विकम्पितुम् अर्हसि – not proper to tremble, धर्म्यात् हि युद्धात् – fighting a righteous war, श्रेय: - better अन्यत - other क्षत्रियस्य – for a kshatriya न – none विद्यते - known

Further, having regard to your own duty, you should not tremble, for there is nothing higher for a Kshatriya than a righteous war. 2-31

Commentary 2-31

Arjuna, look at your duty as a Kshatriya – the warrior whose duty is to fight and protect dharma. For a warrior, there is nothing greater than fighting a righteous war. Having exhausted all diplomatic methods to find a solution, the only course left for the Pandavas is to fight. Holding on to one's swadharma is most important. Therefore, Arjuna is encouraged to fight.

Verse 2-32

यदृच्छया चोपपन्नं स्वर्गद्वारमपावृतम् ।

सुखिनः क्षत्रियाः पार्थ लभन्ते युद्धमीदृशम् ॥ २-३२ ॥

Yadricchayaa chopapannam swargadwaaram apaavritam;

Sukhinah kshatriyaah paartha labhante yuddham eedrisham 2-32

Explanation to Verse 2-32

यत् –this ऋच्छया – from R ऋच्छ to fail in faculties - not by free will but by chance, च – and, उपपन्नं – arisen स्वर्गद्वारम् - gates of heaven अपावृतम् - open up सुखिनः - one who is happy क्षत्रियाः – for a kshatriya पार्थ - O Arjuna लभन्ते – get or benefit युद्धम् –war, ईदृशम् - like this

Happy are the Kshatriyas, O Arjuna, who get the chance to fight in such a battle that comes of itself as an open door to heaven! 2-32

Commentary 2-32

Every person has a duty to perform. Not everybody gets a chance to perform his duty as opportunity does not come to all due to various reasons. How many Kshatriyas get a chance to fight? The Pandavas spent many years in exile roaming around the forests. O Arjuna, you should now think of this war as a great opportunity to fight for a cause. Only the blessed Kshatriyas get such an opportunity that comes as an unsought gateway to heaven.

Verse 2-33

अथ चेत्त्वमिमं धर्म्यं सङ्ग्रामं न करिष्यसि ।
ततः स्वधर्मं कीर्तिं च हित्वा पापमवाप्स्यसि ॥ २-३३॥

Atha chettwam imam dharmyam samgraamam na karishyasi;
Tatah swadharmam keertim cha hitwaa paapam avaapsyasi. 2-33

Explanation to Verse 2-33

अथ- now, चेत् – if, त्वम्-you, इमं- this धर्म्यं - righteous संग्रामं – fighting, war न – not करिष्यसि - perform ततः – then स्वधर्मं – own code of conduct कीर्ति – fame, reputation च – and, हित्वा - abandon पापम् - sin अवाप्स्यसि - you will be engulfed

Now, if you will not fight this righteous war, then, you shall incur sin for having abandoned your (dharmic) duty and lose your fame. 2-33

Commentary 2-33

In the techniques of persuasion, it is not enough if one explains an action that must be done to achieve a result. To be effective, the consequences of not performing a desired action must also be told. What happens if Arjuna does not fight this war? The Lord explains to Arjuna the consequences of not fighting this war. O Arjuna, if you will not fight this righteous war, you will be abandoning your duty and honor. You will only incur sin.

Example: In a company, all workers were required to sign a declaration to accept company's policies. One worker refused. His boss and peers advised him to sign and yet he refused. The CEO called him and told him sternly, "You sign or you are out of your job." He signed immediately. The CEO asked him why he did not sign when his boss asked him. He replied, "Sir, he only told me to sign but did not tell me *the consequence of not signing.* Only you told me clearly and so I signed."

Verse 2-34

अकीर्तिं चापि भूतानि कथयिष्यन्ति तेऽव्ययाम् ।
सम्भावितस्य चाकीर्तिर्मरणादतिरिच्यते ॥ २-३४॥

Akeertim chaapi bhootaani kathayishyanti te'vyayaam;
Sambhaavitasya chaakeertir maranaad atirichyate. 2-34

Explanation to Verse 2-34

अकीर्तिं – defamation, dishonor च – and अपि – too भूतानि – people कथयिष्यन्ति – will speak ते – of you अव्ययाम् – forever (from R व्ययः to spend, diminish) संभावितस्य – for a honorable man (from संभू = to attain esteem) च – and अकीर्तिः - dishonor मरणात्-than death अतिरिच्यते - अति + रिच् - to exceed, more than

People, too, will recount your everlasting dishonour; and to one who is honorable, dishonour is worse than death. 2-34

Commentary 2-34

What will people talk about you? Everybody craves for recognition and praise. If you do not fight, people will talk ill of you and throw permanent dishonor on you. To an honorable person (like you is implied), infamy is surely worse than death. (Note: Heard of *hara-kiri* amongst the Japanese who consider death to be better than dishonor?)

Verse 2-35

भयाद्रणादुपरतं मंस्यन्ते त्वां महारथाः ।

येषां च त्वं बहुमतो भूत्वा यास्यसि लाघवम् ॥ २-३५॥

Bhayaad ranaad uparatam mamsyante twaam mahaarathaah;

Yeshaam cha twam bahumato bhootwaa yaasyasi laaghavam 2-35

Explanation to Verse 2-35

भयात् – out of fear, रणात् – from the battle, उपरतं- उप + रत - run away मंस्यन्ते – will think त्वां – thou महारथाः – the great warriors, येषां – for whom च – also त्वम्- you बहुमत: -बहु (a lot) + मतः (from मन् to think) – think high, held in great esteem, भूत्वा - having been यास्यसि – you will go लाघवम् - (from R लघु - small) - insignificant

The great warriors will think that you have withdrawn from the battle through fear; and you will be considered insignificant by those who had held you in high regard 2-35.

Commentary 2-35

Explaining further, Lord Krishna tells Arjuna, "If you do not fight, the great warriors will think that you are scared and have fled from the war out of fear; To an honorable warrior like you, it will be a great disgrace to be regarded as a coward." (Lesson: Earning a reputation is hard; destroying it is easy)

Verse 2-36

अवाच्यवादांश्च बहून्वदिष्यन्ति तवाहिताः ।

निन्दन्तस्तव सामर्थ्यं ततो दुःखतरं नु किम् ॥ २-३६॥

Avaachyavaadaamshcha bahoon vadishyanti tavaahitaah;

Nindantastava saamarthyam tato duhkhataram nu kim 2-36

Explanation to Verse 2-36

अवाच्यवादान् - न वाच्यः unspeakable + वादान् – words च- and. बहून् – many, वदिष्यन्ति – will speak तव – your अहिताः – अ + हिताः – those ill-disposed; enemiesनिन्दन्तः - denounce, villify तव – your सामर्थ्यं – ability, strength, ततः दुःखतरं नु किम् - what could be more painful?

Thy enemies also, vilifying your power, will speak many abusive words. What is more painful than this! 2-36

Commentary 2-36

Any sensitive person will be provoked by slander and infamy. Krishna continues and says, "O Arjuna, your enemies will slander your superior strength and speak ill of you. What could be more painful than such words?"

Arjuna was a terror and a scorcher of enemies. If he withdraws from war, the enemies will exploit the situation and ridicule him. They may even make jokes on him. It will become unbearable to a great warrior like Arjuna.

Verse 2-37

हतो वा प्राप्स्यसि स्वर्गं जित्वा वा भोक्ष्यसे महीम् ।

तस्मादुत्तिष्ठ कौन्तेय युद्धाय कृतनिश्चयः ॥ २-३७॥

Hato vaa praapsyasi swargam jitwaa vaa bhokshyase maheem;

Tasmaad uttishtha kaunteya yuddhaaya kritanishchayah 2-37

Explanation to Verse 2-37

हत: वा – if killed प्राप्स्यसि – obtain स्वर्गं – heaven जित्वा वा- if won भोक्ष्यसे – enjoy महीम् - the world तस्मात् – therefore, उत्तिष्ठ – get up कौन्तेय- O Arjuna, son of Kunti युद्धाय – to fight कृत – determined निश्चयः – in certainty

If slain, you will obtain heaven; Victorious, you will enjoy the earth; therefore, get up, O son of Kunti, fight with determination! 2-37

Commentary 2-37

So, Arjuna, son of Kunti, decide now to fight. If you get killed in the war, you will attain heaven (as you have done your duty as a Kshatriya); If you win, you will enjoy this world. Thus, Lord Krishna advances his argument on why Arjuna should fight this war and what are the likely consequences if he does not fight. In the next verse, he tells him how he should perform this task.

Verse 2-38

सुखदुःखे समे कृत्वा लाभालाभौ जयाजयौ ।

ततो युद्धाय युज्यस्व नैवं पापमवाप्स्यसि ॥ २-३८॥

Sukhaduhkhe same' kritwaa laabha alaabhau jaya ajayau;

Tato yuddhaaya yujyaswa naivam paapama vaapsyasi 2-38

Explanation to Verse 2-38

सुखदुःखे - सुखम् च दुःखं च (N, S) - in happiness and grief समे – from सम - equal, कृत्वा – R कृ to do – Having done लाभ- gain, (अ)लाभौ – loss,जय- victory,(अ)जय-defeat तत: -then युद्धाय – in battle, युज्यस्व – join (R –yuj), न एवं पापम् अवाप्स्यसि - you will not incur sin

Having made pleasure and pain, gain and loss, victory and defeat the same, *(only)* then engage in battle for the sake of battle; thus thou shalt not incur sin. 2-38

Commentary 2-38

Killing is not pleasant. How does Arjuna perform a duty that is unpleasant?

It is performed with a different frame of mind. Lord Krishna talks about the attitude one should adopt in performing one's duty. This advice, coming from the Lord, is not only for Arjuna but to everyone. It is a LESSON. There are many events in our world that are liked and disliked by people. By treating pain and pleasure in the same way, the mind become steady and stronger. It is a matter of adopting 'Samatvam' or equanimity – an attitude of mental calmness, composure, and evenness of temper, especially in a difficult situation. Lord Krishna exhorts Arjuna to adopt such an attitude and treat alike pain and pleasure, gain and loss, victory and defeat in fighting this war. By treating success and failure alike, one develops a healthy mental disposition and does not incur sin. The important lesson here is to face difficult situations in life boldly unmindful of the outcome.

Verse 2-39

एषा तेऽभिहिता साङ्ख्ये बुद्धिर्योगे त्विमां श्रृणु ।
बुद्ध्या युक्तो यया पार्थ कर्मबन्धं प्रहास्यसि ॥ २-३९ ॥

Eshaa te'abhihitaa saankhye buddhir yoge twimaam shrinu;
Buddhyaa yukto yayaa paartha karma bandham prahaasyasi.2-39

Explanation to Verse 2-39

एषा – this ते - for you अभिहिता – said, spoken, सांख्ये- concerning Sankhya wisdom बुद्धि: - to know, intelligence, योगे – concerning Yoga, तु इमां श्रृणु - (त्वम्) इमां श्रृणु – listen to this, बुद्ध्या – with knowledge. युक्त: – making use of, endowed यया – you, पार्थ – O'Arjuna. कर्मबन्धं- bondage of action, प्रहास्यसि – cast off

This which has been taught to you, is the wisdom concerning Sankhya. Now listen to the wisdom concerning Yoga, endowed with which, O' Arjuna, thou shall cast off the bonds of action! 2-39

Commentary 2-39

Self-discovery *or 'Atma-Jnanam'* is referred here as *'Saamkhya.'* What is Saamkhya? It is one of the six systems of philosophy in Sanaatana Dharma – popularly known as Hinduism. Lord Krishna uses the word Saamkhya here to mean self-discovery. It means the discovery of the truth that you can be independent and free from external sources to be happy. The basic principles of self-knowledge including a description of Atma are already presented (verses 11-39). But the subject of Atma is highly philosophical and knowing the self is not easy for a common man to comprehend and therefore, a step is required to make it easier. This step is the Karma Yoga. Having explained this self-knowledge (also referred as Jnana Yoga), Lord Krishna now moves on to the next important topic for learning – the Karma Yoga.

In the following verses, Lord Krishna teaches the fundamentals of Karma Yoga. He tells Arjuna that he, armed with the knowledge of Karma Yoga, will be able to break through the bonds of Karma (*karmabandham prahasyasi*).

Verse 2-40

नेहाभिक्रमनाशोऽस्ति प्रत्यवायो न विद्यते ।
स्वल्पमप्यस्य धर्मस्य त्रायते महतो भयात् ॥ २-४० ॥

Neha abhikramanaasho'sti pratyavaayo na vidyate;
Swalpam apyasya dharmasya traayate mahato bhayaat 2-40

Explanation to Verse 2-40

नेहाभिक्रमनाशोऽस्ति = न इह अभिक्रमनाशः अस्ति= न इह –Not, here, - अभि + क्रम् – begin + sequence, नाशः destruction, अस्ति-is; प्रत्यवायः = प्रति + अव + अय् - contrary or negative result, न no विद्यते - exists or possible, स्वल्पं – little, अपि – even, अस्य – this (yoga), धर्मस्य – of dharma (righteous conduct), त्रायते – protects, महतः – great, भयात - from fear.

In this there is no loss of effort, nor is there any negative impact (destruction). Even a little of this Yoga protects one from great fear. 2-40

Commentary 2-40

Lord Krishna begins with an assurance that in the field of Karma Yoga there is no failure or adverse result. Even a partial practice of this Yoga produces results and protects one from the great fear. It comes as a wonderful remedy. It seems to be a sure success method to resolve one's problems. Krishna glorifies the Karma Yoga. What is this great Yoga? Details follow.

Verse 2-41

व्यवसायात्मिका बुद्धिरेकेह कुरुनन्दन ।

बहुशाखा ह्यनन्ताश्च बुद्धयोऽव्यवसायिनाम् ॥ २-४१ ॥

 Vyavasaayaatmikaa buddhir ekeha kurunandana;

Bahushaakhaa hyanantaashcha buddhayo'vyavasaayinaam. 2-41

Explanation to Verse 2-41

व्यवसायात्मिका = व्यवसायः + आत्मा – determination + self, बुद्धिः - intelligence एका – one इह – here, कुरुनन्दन – joyful son of the Kuru family बहुशाखा: - many branches, हि- indeed अनन्ता: - endless, च – and बुद्धयः –

intelligence अव्यवसायिनाम् - one who lacks determination, has wavering mind, irresolute

Here, O joy of the Kurus, (for the intelligent) there is a single one-pointed determination! Many-branched and endless are the thoughts of the irresolute 2-41

Commentary 2-41

Arjuna is addressed with a new name – *Kurunandana* – the joy of the Kurus.

In life, we all face different problems. To address them, many options are prescribed by different people. One gets bewildered by the sheer number of such options. People often get distressed by trying out different options. Karma Yoga is strengthening the mind and get a clear idea of what to follow. Steady mind comes to the one who learns concentration. It is like shooting an arrow at a target. Most rituals or *'saadhanas'* to attain purity of mind and steadying it will fall under Karma Yoga.

A person who practices Karma Yoga is called Karma Yogi. He works with one-pointed determination and clearly knows his goal and priorities. Those with unsteady mind get confused with many multi-branched thoughts unable to reach a decision. Clarity of thoughts and concentration are essential to be happy. Karma Yoga facilitates the process to reach such a quality.

Verse 2-42

यामिमां पुष्पितां वाचं प्रवदन्त्यविपश्चितः ।
वेदवादरताः पार्थ नान्यदस्तीति वादिनः ॥ २-४२ ॥

Yaam imaam pushpitaam vaacham pravadantya avipashchitah;
Vedavaadarataah paartha naanyad asteeti vaadinah.2-42

Explanation to Verse 2-42

यामिमां = यां इमां – which, this, पुष्पितां – flowery, वाचं – speech, प्रवदन्ति – utter अविपश्चितः = न विपश्चित् – not wise person, वेदवादरताः - taking pleasure in the eulogising words of the *Vedas* पार्थ – O' Arjuna न – nothing अन्यत् – else अस्ति – is इति – so वादिनः saying

Flowery speech is uttered by the unwise, who take pleasure in the eulogising words of the *Vedas,* O Arjuna, saying: "There is nothing else!" 2-42

Commentary 2-42

We see and hear many people talking sweetly but selfish and materialistic. They are called *'avipaschitaha'* meaning unwise; *avivekah* – lacking discrimination. They lack intelligence and discrimination because they think that materialistic gains can make their lives happy and successful. Such people also misinterpret the holy Vedas and take pleasure in eulogizing some words of the Vedas. Pursuing material needs are not opposed by the Vedas but they also prescribe spiritual and emotional growth through certain practices. The LESSON here is that even though money is required to buy many material things like a nice bed or a luxury home, it cannot guarantee to provide good sleep or genuine love. Lord Krishna criticizes such people.

Verse 2-43

कामात्मानः स्वर्गपरा जन्मकर्मफलप्रदाम् ।
क्रियाविशेषबहुलां भोगैश्वर्यगतिं प्रति ॥ २-४३ ॥

Kaamaatmaanah swargaparaa janmakarma phalapradaam;
Kriyaa vishesha bahulaam bhogai aishwarya gatim prati.2-43

Explanation to Verse 2-43

काम-आत्मानः – full of desires स्वर्गपरा:- with heaven as their goal जन्मकर्मफलप्रदाम् – birth as the reward of one's actions क्रियाविशेषबहुलां = क्रियायाः + विशेषः + बहुलाम् –actions +specific + multifold -भोग- pleasures ऐश्वर्य = ईश्वरस्य इदं इति ऐश्वर्यम् - power, गतिं - go प्रति - towards

Full of desires, having heaven as their goal, they utter speech which promises birth as the reward of one's actions, and prescribe various specific actions for the attainment of pleasure and power. 2-43

Commentary 2-43

Most people are driven by materialistic and sensory desires (*kaamatatmanah*). The highest goal they have is *svargapara* – attainment of heaven. To achieve this goal, they will undertake various specific actions (*vishesha bahulaam*). The ultimate purpose is to reap pleasure and lordship to satisfy their desires. Where does all their actions lead to? To new birth because of their work (*janma karma phala pradaam*).

Verse 2-44

भोगैश्वर्यप्रसक्तानां तयापहृतचेतसाम् ।

व्यवसायात्मिका बुद्धिः समाधौ न विधीयते ॥ २-४४॥

Bhogaishwarya prasaktaanaam tayaa pahrita chetasaam;
Vyavasaaya atmikaa buddhih samaadhau na vidheeyate. 2-44

Explanation to Verse 2-44

भोग-ऐश्वर्य- pleasures and power, प्रसक्तानां = प्र + सच् - to enjoy, + immersed, तया – those, अपहृतचेतसाम्- of distracted mind and intellect, व्यवसायात्मिका - focused intellect or determinate faculty बुद्धिः –

intelligence समाधौ – in Samadhi (the state of super consciousness) न –not, विधीयते - manifested

For those who are much attached to pleasure and power, whose minds are distracted away by those (desires), the determinate faculty on meditation and super consciousness is not manifested 2-44

Commentary 2-44

Lord Krishna continues to talk about those people who cling to pleasures and powers. For them, discrimination (viveka) gets eroded, and mind becomes unsteady. Arising out of desires and greed, we see many people losing a sense of honesty and becoming corrupt. This undesirable quality is described in this verse as *apahrtachetasam*.

Verse 2-45

त्रैगुण्यविषया वेदा निस्त्रैगुण्यो भवार्जुन ।

निर्द्वन्द्वो नित्यसत्त्वस्थो निर्योगक्षेम आत्मवान्॥ २-४५॥

Traigunyavishayaa vedaa nis traigunyo bhavaarjuna;
Nirdwandwo nityasatwastho niryogakshema aatmavaan. 2-45

Explanation to Verse 2-45

त्रैगुण्यविषया: = गुणानां त्रयम् – (सत्त्व **the noble,** रजस् **the average,** तमस् **the lowly)** – the trinity of attributes, वेदा:- the Vedas, निस्त्रैगुण्य: भव अर्जुन – be above the three attributes O' Arjuna, निर्द्वन्द्व: - Free yourself from the pairs of opposites, नित्यसत्त्वस्थ: - remain ever in Satwa निर्योगक्षेम: - without thoughts of (personal) happiness आत्मवान् - focused on the soul

The Vedas mention the three attributes: be thou above these three attributes, O Arjuna! Free yourself from the pairs of opposites and ever remain in Satwa, freed from the thought of personal welfare, focused on the Self.2-45

Commentary 2-45

How should one go about following Karma Yoga? Lord Krishna answers this question in a simple way citing the Vedas. Vedas describe three Gunas or attributes that generally cover pursuit of material activities. Contrary to a common perception, Vedas are not against materialistic pursuits and enjoying pleasures. One who follows Karma Yoga should not give undue importance to material pursuits and get carried away by such pleasures. Lord Krishna advises Arjuna – *Nistraigunyo Bhava* – be free (from the desires arising) from the three Gunas. Further, a Karma Yogi should be able to bear patiently the ups and downs (opposites like rich/poor, hot/cold) in life (*nirdvandvo bhava*). A supplementary quality that a Karma Yogi should have is to maintain Satva Guna (*Nityasattvashto*) – an attribute to have the power of discrimination and strength of mind. Such a quality can be best developed by acquiring knowledge through various scriptures and/or associating with great spiritually minded Gurus and Mahaans. Lastly, a Karma Yogi must be ever alert not to be blown away by trying situations in life. He should constantly be aware of his goal in life and move towards achieving it. Thus, Lord Krishna sums up the fundamentals of Karma Yoga

Verse 2-46

यावानर्थ उदपाने सर्वतः सम्प्लुतोदके ।

तावान्सर्वेषु वेदेषु ब्राह्मणस्य विजानतः ॥ २-४६ ॥

Yaavaanartha udapaane sarvatah samplu todake;
Taavaan sarveshu vedeshu braahmanasya vijaanatah. 2-46

Explanation to Verse 2-46

यावान् = यावत् - similar to, just as अर्थ: - meaning उदपाने = उदपान – pond सर्वत: – from all sides संप्लुतोदके = संप्लुते उदके - flood of water तावान् = तावत् - like that सर्वेषु – all, वेदेषु- the Vedas, ब्राह्मणस्य - follower of Brahman – one who has attained super consciousness, विजानत: - वि + ज्ञा - known

To the Brahmana who has known the Self, all the *Vedas* are of as much use as is a pond of water in a place where there is a flood. 2-46

Commentary 2-46

How does Karma Yoga benefit someone who practices it in the way described in the earlier verse? It leads to infinite bliss. To the wise, it is so encompassing that the benefit of all worldly pleasures obtained through the Vedas seem as useful as the water procured from a tank when there is flood everywhere. In other words, the infinite bliss or Moksha includes all finite pleasures too.

Verse 2-47

कर्मण्येवाधिकारस्ते मा फलेषु कदाचन ।

मा कर्मफलहेतुर्भूर्मा ते सङ्गोऽस्त्वकर्मणि ॥ २-४७॥

Karmanyeva adhikaaraste maa phaleshu kadaachana;

Maa karma phalahetur bhoor maa te sango' astwakarmani. 2-47

Explanation to Verse 2-47

कर्मणि – work, एव - only अधिकार: - अधि + कृ – authority, right ते –to, मा - not फलेषु- fruits, results कदाचन – never मा कर्मफलहेतु: - कर्मण:+ फलं + हेतु: - actions + fruits + cause or motive भू: – being/having सङ्ग: - सम् + गम् – going with, attachment , अकर्मणि - inaction, मा ते अस्तु - May you not

Your right is to work only, but never with its fruits; let not the fruits of actions be your motive, nor let your attachment be to inaction 2-47

Commentary 2-47

This verse is often quoted as a key verse in Bhagavad Gita. It describes Karma Yoga in a nutshell. It provides a new perspective to Karma Yoga. Most people work with expectations of a reward. When they do not get the expected reward, they get totally disappointed or demotivated. Lord Krishna advises Arjuna – You have a right or freedom to choose the action you wish to do. But you have no right regarding the fruits (results) of it. With all actions to achieve a goal, sometimes it may not yield the results one seeks. You may plan intelligently, work hard towards a goal but there are many factors like weather, political changes, floods, accidents and several others that are beyond your control. So, ultimately, you can only hope for the best. The MESSAGE here is – Perform your actions but if you get results different from your expectations, learn to accept it without getting demotivated; Let not your motive be the fruits of your action. At the same time, do not resort to inaction because of you failed to get the fruits. In other words, strengthen your mind to accept things that you do not expect; perform your duty unmindful of the results.

How does a person work without desire and live in this competitive world?

Lord Krishna goes on to explain further on Karma Yoga and the benefits arising from practising it.

Verse 2-48

योगस्थः कुरु कर्माणि सङ्गं त्यक्त्वा धनञ्जय ।

सिद्ध्यसिद्ध्योः समो भूत्वा समत्वं योग उच्यते ॥२-४८॥

Yogasthah kuru karmaani sangam tyaktwaa dhananjaya;
Siddhyasiddhyoh samo bhootwaa samatwam yoga uchyate. 2-48

Explanation to Verse 2-48

योगस्थः = योगे तिष्ठति इति योगस्थः (स्था to stop) steadied in yoga, कुरु- perform, कर्माणि – action, सङ्गं – attachment, bond त्यक्त्वा – (R त्यज्) abandoning, धनंजय – O' Arjuna (one has won wealth/glory), सिद्धि-असिद्ध्योः –in success and failure समः भूत्वा – balanced समत्वं योगः उच्यते – such equanimity is called Yoga!

Perform action, O Arjuna, being steadfast in Yoga, abandoning attachment and balanced in success and failure! Such equanimity is called Yoga. 2-48

Commentary 2.48

O' Arjuna (addressed as Dhananjaya), therefore, perform action by being steadfast in yoga, renouncing material attachments; by being even minded in both success and failure as mental equilibrium is the essence of yoga.

A karma yogi places importance on spiritual growth and holds all activities as ordained by the Lord. He does not get elated by success nor cries over failure. He remains equanimous in both success (siddhi) and failure (asiddhi).

Such an even-minded attitude is verily called Karma Yoga (*samatvam yogah uchyate*). Lord Krishna is advising Arjuna to develop such a poise of mind. This applies to all of us too.

Verse 2-49

दूरेण ह्यवरं कर्म बुद्धियोगाद्धनञ्जय ।
बुद्धौ शरणमन्विच्छ कृपणाः फलहेतवः ॥ २-४९ ॥

Doorena hyavaram karma buddhiyogaad dhananjaya;
Buddhau sharanamanwiccha kripanaah phalahetavah. 2-49

Explanation to Verse 2-49

दूरेण – far, हि, certainly, अवरं – not desirable, कर्म – action, बुद्धियोगात् – the Yoga of Wisdom, धनंजय- O Arjuna! बुद्धौ शरणम् - Take refuge in wisdom, अन्विच्छ - अनु + इष् desire or seek, कृपणाः – misers, wretched, फलहेतवः – फलस्य – fruit, हेतुः - reason, motive

Far lower than the Yoga of wisdom is action *(motivated by results)*, O Arjuna! Seek thou refuge in wisdom; wretched are they whose motive is the fruit. 2-49

Commentary 2-49

Karma Yoga considers that working purely with a specific motive is inferior to its ideals. An average person works for a wage or material rewards. He gives importance only to material accomplishments. Karma Yoga highlights attitude, poise and wisdom, it is also called *Buddhiyoga.* Lord Krishna says - O'Arjuna, adopt Buddhiyoga – balanced attitude. Those who are motivated only by results are wretched. So, take the path of Karma Yoga.

MESSAGE: Pride in one's work is very important. An example: When the author was in Japan, he witnessed a 'quality circle' of rest room attendants. They formed the circle on their own and made sure that the toilets were kept clean and shining without looking for any reward. They felt proud about the work;The best part was that all of them were seniors above the age of sixty!

Verse 2-50

बुद्धियुक्तो जहातीह उभे सुकृतदुष्कृते ।

तस्माद्योगाय युज्यस्व योगः कर्मसु कौशलम् ॥ २-५० ॥

Buddhiyukto jahaateeha ubhe sukrita dushkrite;
Tasmaad yogaaya yujyaswa yogah karmasu kaushalam.2-50

Explanation to Verse 2-50

बुद्धियुक्तः = बुद्ध्या युक्तः - Endowed with wisdom, जहाति – casts off, इह – in this life, उभे – both, सुकृतदुष्कृते = सुकृतं च दुष्कृतं च - good and evil deeds, तस्मात् – therefore, योगाय - to yoga, युज्यस्व – from the R युज्, join, devote. योगः – Yoga, कर्मस, in action, कौशलम् - skill

Endowed with wisdom (evenness of mind), one casts off in this life both good and evil deeds; therefore, devote thyself to Yoga; Yoga is skill in action 2-50

Commentary 2-50

This verse supplements what is already said in the earlier verse. A karmayogi (referred to *as buddhiyuktaha*-endowed with wisdom) having a balanced mind frees himself from vice and virtues (*punyam and paapam*) alike here itself. Mental poise comes only when one is free from likes and dislikes, attachments and hate. He gains peace of mind. Therefore, devote yourself to following this (karma) yoga that works efficiently with proper attitudinal skills.

Verse 2-51

कर्मजं बुद्धियुक्ता हि फलं त्यक्त्वा मनीषिणः ।
जन्मबन्धविनिर्मुक्ताः पदं गच्छन्त्यनामयम् ॥ २-५१ ॥

Karmajam buddhiyuktaa hi phalam tyaktwaa maneeshinah;
Janmabandha vinirmuktaah padam gacchantyanaamayam. 2-51

Explanation to Verse 2-51

कर्मजं – action born, बुद्धियुक्ताः those possessed with intellect, हि- indeed, of course फलं त्यक्त्वा - having abandoned the fruits, मनीषिणः –

the wise जन्मबन्धविनिर्–मुक्ताः - freed from the fetters of birth, पदं- the abode, गच्छन्ति - go to, अनामयम् -beyond all evil.

The wise, possessed of knowledge, having abandoned the fruits of their actions, and being freed from the fetters of birth, go to the place which is beyond all evil.2-51

Commentary 2-51

Imbued with a balanced mind, the knowledgeable people do not attach importance to material benefits, nor do they crave for fruits of their actions. Having given up the results born of their actions; the karma yogis become wise. Thus, they get freed from the fetters of rebirth and attain that state free from evil.

Verse 2-52

यदा ते मोहकलिलं बुद्धिर्व्यतितरिष्यति ।
तदा गन्तासि निर्वेदं श्रोतव्यस्य श्रुतस्य च ॥ २-५२ ॥

 Yadaa te mohakalilam buddhir vyatitarishyati;
Tadaa gantaasi nirvedam shrotavyasya shrutasya cha.2-52

Explanation to Verse 2-52

यदा – when, ते – your, मोह-कलिलं - मोहस्य of delusion कलिलम् - dense, बुद्धिः – intellect, व्यतितरिष्यति - R वि + अति + तृ (to cross) इति – crosses, surpasses, तदा – then गन्ता असि - one who goes or attains, निर्वेदं - being unconcerned or indifferent, श्रोतव्यस्य- of what is yet to be heard, श्रुतस्य- of what is heard in the past, च - and

When your intellect crosses beyond the mire of delusion, then you shall attain indifference to what has been heard and what is yet to be heard 2-52

Commentary 2-52

One of the benefits of Karma Yoga is that it helps to get clarity in the thinking process. A karma yogi is better positioned to understand the Atma, control of senses, the Real and the unreal. The understanding helps to develop dispassion and become indifferent to things heard and unheard. He becomes an independent thinker.

Verse 2-53

श्रुतिविप्रतिपन्ना ते यदा स्थास्यति निश्चला ।

समाधावचला बुद्धिस्तदा योगमवाप्स्यसि ॥ २-५३॥

Shrutivipratipannaa te yadaa sthaasyati nishchalaa;
Samaadhaavachalaa buddhistadaa yogam avaapsyasi. 2-53

Explanation to Verse 2-53

श्रुतिविप्रतिपन्ना = श्रुति – What is heard - Vedic revelation + विप्रतिपन्ना – perplexed by, ते – thy, यदा – when, स्थास्यति – stand, निश्चला - निः + चल्-immovable, समाधौ – in the Self, अचला – steady बुद्धिः – intellect, तदा – then योगं - Self-realization, अवाप्स्यसि - attain

When your intellect, perplexed by what you have heard, shall stand immovable and steady in the Self, then you shalt attain Self-realisation. 2-53

Commentary 2-53

An average person is often tossed about by mental conflicts. However, when the intellect becomes poised and firm (*achala tishtati*). With such a mental state, one is said to attain Yoga.

With this verse, Lord Krishna has concluded his teaching on Karma Yoga.

Verse 2-54

अर्जुन उवाच ।

स्थितप्रज्ञस्य का भाषा समाधिस्थस्य केशव ।

स्थितधीः किं प्रभाषेत किमासीत व्रजेत किम् ॥२- ५४॥

Arjuna Uvaacha:

Sthitaprajnasya kaa bhaashaa
samaadhisthasya keshava;

Sthita dheeh kim prabhaasheta
kimaaseeta vrajeta kim. 2-54

Explanation to Verse 2-54

अर्जुनः उवाच - Arjuna said: स्थितप्रज्ञस्य = स्थिता प्रज्ञा यस्य सः - one who has steady wisdom का – what, भाषा- description, समाधिस्थस्य - merged in the Superconscious State, केशव - O Krishna, स्थितधीः - one of steady wisdom किं – how, प्रभाषेत – does he speak, किम् – How, आसीत – does he sit व्रजेत – walk, किम् – how

Arjuna said: O Krishna, what is the description of one who has steady wisdom and is merged in the Superconscious State? How does one of steady wisdom speak? How does he sit? How does he walk? 2-54

Commentary 2-54

After hearing Lord Krishna, Arjuna now gets an opportunity to respond with his questions.

Arjuna asked – O' Krishna (Keshava), what is the mark of a wise man who has established himself in the 'Self?' Tell me how such a person speaks, sits and walks?

The word *'Sthithaprajna'* is used here to describe a person who is free from any confusion, having clear knowledge, steady in mind, and full of conviction. Arjuna is curious to know the traits of such a person.

Verse 2-55

श्रीभगवानुवाच ।

प्रजहाति यदा कामान्सर्वान्पार्थ मनोगतान् ।

आत्मन्येवात्मना तुष्टः स्थितप्रज्ञस्तदोच्यते ॥ २-५५॥

Sri Bhagavaan Uvaacha:

Prajahaati yadaa kaamaan   sarvaan paartha manogataan;

Aatmany evaatmanaa tushtah   sthita-prajnas tado uchyate. 2-55

Explanation to Verse 2-55

प्रजहाति – gives up, यदा – when, कामान् – desires for sense gratification, सर्वान् – all, पार्थ – O'Arjuna, मनोगतान् - of the mind, as the mind goes, आत्मनि – in the Self, एव – only, आत्मना – by the Self, तुष्टः – satisfied, स्थितप्रज्ञः - of steady wisdom, तदा – then, उच्यते - said to be.

The Blessed Lord said:

When a man completely casts off, O Arjuna, all the desires of the mind and is satisfied in the Self by the Self, then is he said to be one of steady wisdom! 2-55

Commentary 2-55

Lord Krishna (Sri Bhagavan) encourages Arjuna to ask questions and replies to him in detail.

The first trait (*lakshanam*) of a Jnani (the wise) as *'Atmani Eva Atmana Tustah'* – meaning one who is happy with himself. No matter what his condition is, he does not seek happiness from outside. This is an important trait of a person with steady wisdom. For him, Atma

(Self) is Bliss. When he is full of self-generated happiness, he has no desires for his internal happiness comes by abandoning desires.

So, when a man abandons desires, and is happy with himself, he is said to be '*sthithaprajnyah*' - a person with steady wisdom.

Verse 2-56

दुःखेष्वनुद्विग्नमनाः सुखेषु विगतस्पृहः ।
वीतरागभयक्रोधः स्थितधीर्मुनिरुच्यते ॥ २-५६ ॥

Duhkheshwa anudvigna manaah

sukheshu vigata sprihah;

Veetaraaga bhayakrodhah   sthitadheer munir uchyate. 2-56

Explanation to Verse 2-56

दुःखेषु – in adversity, अनुद्विग्नमनाः = न उद्विग्नम् + मनः – not shaken or distressed, in mind सुखेषु – in pleasures, विगतस्पृहः = विगता + स्पृहा - gone + to desire, वीतरागभयक्रोधः = वीतः + रागः च भयं च क्रोधः – free from attachment, fear and anger, स्थितधीः – of steady wisdom, मुनिः – sage , उच्यते – is called

He whose mind is not shaken by adversity, who does not hanker after pleasures, and who is free from attachment, fear and anger, is called a sage of steady wisdom.2-56

Commentary 2-56

In real world, we all go through ups and downs in life. How does a person with a steady mind face different difficult situations in life?

The person of wisdom remains unperturbed by adversity. He does not crave for happiness accepting life as it comes. He remains unconcerned with objects of pleasure, is free from attachment, and from emotions like anger and fear.

A person possessing such qualities is said to be a sage of steady wisdom.

Verse 2-57

यः सर्वत्रानभिस्नेहस्तत्तत्प्राप्य शुभाशुभम् ।
नाभिनन्दति न द्वेष्टि तस्य प्रज्ञा प्रतिष्ठिता ॥ २-५७॥

Yah sarvatraanabhisnehas tat tat praapya shubhaashubham;
Naabhinandati na dweshti tasya prajnaa pratishthitaa.2-57

Explanation to Verse 2-57

यः - He who, सर्वत्र - everywhere अनभिस्नेहः = अन् + अभिस्नेहः – (**R** स्निह् – to feel, have affection), without attachment, तत् - that तत् – that, प्राप्य – having obtained, शुभ-अशुभम् - good or bad न – not, अभिनन्दति – rejoices, न – not, द्वेष्टि – hates, तस्य – his प्रज्ञा – wisdom, प्रतिष्ठिता – is fixed

He who is everywhere without attachment, on meeting with anything good or bad, who neither rejoices nor hates, his wisdom is fixed. 2-57

Commentary 2-57

We all face moments of joy and sorrow. It is a part of life. How does an average person react to such situations? He may celebrate the joy through various means – drinking, feasting, entertainment and so on. On the other hand, sorrow may bring tears and pain in the heart. Some people cry, share their sorrow to others by lamenting or just move about silently. In contrast, the jnani (the wise) is unattached (*anabhisnehaah*) everywhere. He is above the turbulence caused by joy or sorrow. He neither rejoices nor hates joyous and sad situations. He always maintains his mental poise and remains firm in wisdom.

Verse 2-58

यदा संहरते चायं कूर्मोऽङ्गानीव सर्वशः ।

इन्द्रियाणीन्द्रियार्थेभ्यस्तस्य प्रज्ञा प्रतिष्ठिता ॥ २-५८॥

Yadaa samharate chaayam kurmo'ngaaneeva sarvashah;

Indriyaaneendriyaarthebhyas   tasya prajnaa pratishthitaa. 2-58

Explanation to Verse 2-58

यदा – when, संहरते – withdraws, च – also अयं – he, कूर्म- tortoise, अङ्गानि – limbs, इव – like, सर्वशः – all sides, इन्द्रियाणि – senses, इन्द्रियार्थेभ्यः – from the sense objects, तस्य – his, प्रज्ञा – consciousness, wisdom, प्रतिष्ठिता - becomes steady.

When, like the tortoise which withdraws its limbs on all sides, he withdraws his senses from the sense-objects, then his wisdom becomes steady. 2-58

Illustration to Verse 2-58

Like the tortoise with limbs on all sides, retracts his limbs from the sense-objects around!

Commentary 2-58

How does a person acquire such remarkable mastery over emotions and remain poised in all situations? Lord Krishna explains further in this and subsequent verse. In this verse, He provides an interesting example of a tortoise. A tortoise does not have any limb – like a horn, or claws, or teeth -to resist an attack. The only defence it has is a hard back. So, when the tortoise senses any danger, it pulls its five limbs (the head and four legs) under its back shell. Likewise, a wise person withdraws his five senses when sensing dangers arising from sense-objects that have the potential to produce desire, anger and hate that in turn create mental turmoil.

This verse tells us the importance of controlling one's senses. Mastery over the senses is a remarkable trait of a jnani-the enlightened one!

Verse 2-59

विषया विनिवर्तन्ते निराहारस्य देहिनः ।

रसवर्जं रसोऽप्यस्य परं दृष्ट्वा निवर्तते ॥ २-५९ ॥

Vishayaa vinivartante niraahaarasya dehinah

Rasavarjam raso'pyasya param drishtwaa nivartate. 2-59

Explanation to Verse 2-59

विषया – objects for enjoyment, विनिवर्तन्ते – turn away, निराहारस्य – abstinent, देहिनः – for the embodied (the man), रसवर्जं – leaving the longing, रसः – taste, longing, अपि – also, अस्य – his, परं –the supreme, दृष्ट्वा – seeing, निवर्तते – turns away

The objects of the senses turn away from the abstinent man, leaving the longing behind; but his longing also turns away on seeing the Supreme 2-59

Commentary 2-59

Continuing further, Lord Krishna says that sense objects (that attract) turn away from creating an impact on a person who has renounced them. However, in some, the mental longing for such objects may persist. Such longing also ceases once he has seen (experienced) the Supreme (param dhristvaa).

Verse 2-60

यततो ह्यपि कौन्तेय पुरुषस्य विपश्चितः ।

इन्द्रियाणि प्रमाथीनि हरन्ति प्रसभं मनः ॥ २-६० ॥

Yatato hyapi kaunteya purushasya vipashchitah;
Indriyaani pramaatheeni haranti prasabham
manah.2-60

Explanation to Verse 2-60

यततः – **(R** यत् – to strive, work hard,) of the striving, हि – indeed, certainly, अपि – even, in spite of, कौन्तेय- O Arjuna, पुरुषस्य – of a man, विपश्चितः – of the wise, इन्द्रियाणि – the senses, प्रमाथीनि – turbulent, हरन्ति- carry away, प्रसभं – forcefully, violently, मनः the mind

The turbulent senses, O Arjuna, do violently carry away the mind of a wise man though he be striving (to control them)! 2-60

Commentary 2-60

O'Arjuna, the nature of uncontrolled senses is such that it can forcibly pull even a wise person who is trying to attain perfection. *'Indriyaani Pramaathini'* means the sense organs are like churner in a mixer or blender – so turbulent. Lord Krishna cautions that it is not easy to control them. Spiritual discipline means battling with the senses and controlling them effectively. '

MESSAGE: *The practice of Karma Yoga offers an opportunity to discipline the mind and body.*

Verse 2-61

तानि सर्वाणि संयम्य युक्त आसीत मत्परः ।

वशो हि यस्येन्द्रियाणि तस्य प्रज्ञा प्रतिष्ठिता ॥ २-६१॥

Taani sarvaani samyamya yukta aaseeta matparah;

Vashe hi yasyendriyaani tasya prajnaa pratishthitaa. 2-61

Explanation to Verse 2-61

तानि – them, सर्वाणि – all *(both pronouns connecting the previous verse and referring to senses)*, संयम्य – having restrained, युक्तः- joined, आसीत – should be, मत्परः – intent on me,वशो – under control, हि – indeed, यस्य – whose, इन्द्रियाणि – senses, तस्य – his प्रज्ञा – wisdom, consciousness, प्रतिष्ठिता - steadfast

Having restrained them all he should sit steadfast, intent on Me; his wisdom is steady whose senses are under control. 2-61

Commentary 2-61

Mind is like a monkey. It keeps jumping constantly with different thoughts. Considering this nature of the mind and how strong the sense organs are, O'Arjuna, keep them restrained and under control. How to do it? Lord Krishna provides guidance. Sit focused on me like a yogi. If the mind gets occupied by divine thoughts in meditation, you can avoid the conflicts in the mind. This way of disciplining the mind is called *Atma Dhyanam* or Self Meditation.

Verse 2-62

ध्यायतो विषयान्पुंसः सङ्गस्तेषूपजायते ।

सङ्गात्सञ्जायते कामः कामात्क्रोधोऽभिजायते॥ २-६२॥

Dhyaayato vishayaan pumsah sangas teshu upajaayate;

Sangaat sanjaayate kaamah kaamaat krodho abhijaayate.2-62

Explanation to Verse 2-62

ध्यायतः – thinks of, विषयान् – (P) objects of the senses, पुंसः – (M) of a man, सङ्गः – attachment, तेषु – to them (pronoun to विषयान्), उपजायते – उप (near) + जायते (from R जन् to be born) – arises, सङ्गात् – from attachment, संजायते – is born, कामः – desire, कामात्- from desire, क्रोधः – anger, अभिजायते – manifests

(The prefixes उप, सम् and अभि indicate progressive increases)

When a man thinks of the objects, attachment to them arises; from attachment desire is born; from desire anger arises. 2-62

Commentary 2-62

However, as mind wanders, most people continue to brood over many objects of senses. What happens when mind keeps thinking about sense objects? It becomes a matter of habit, and a person develops attachments to the sense objects – like the drumming of TV commercials impact the senses and thus influence the mind of the viewers to desire a product. From attachment comes desire. If the desire is not fulfilled, it turns into anger. And anger may eventually turn into a crime.

Verse 2-63

क्रोधाद्भवति सम्मोहः सम्मोहात्स्मृतिविभ्रमः ।

स्मृतिभ्रंशाद् बुद्धिनाशो बुद्धिनाशात्प्रणश्यति ॥२-६३॥

Krodhaad bhavati sammohah sammohaat smriti vibhramah;

Smriti bhramshaad buddhi naasho buddhi naashaat pranashyati 2-63

Explanation to Verse 2-63

क्रोधात् – from anger, भवति - comes संमोहः - delusion संमोहात् - from delusion, स्मृतिविभ्रमः, loss of memory; स्मृतिभ्रंशात् - from loss of memory, बुद्धिनाशः- loss of intelligence, बुद्धिनाशात् - from the destruction of intelligence, प्रणश्यति - he perishes

From anger comes delusion; from delusion the loss of memory; from loss of memory the destruction of intelligence; from the destruction of intelligence, he perishes.2-63

Commentary 2-63

Lord Krishna continues to explain the sequence of impacts caused by a man's lack of control on senses. Unfulfilled desire leads to anger. In turn, anger causes more harmful effects. From anger arises delusion (*sammohaha*). Delusion leads to loss of memory and confusion; that in turn results in the destruction of the power of discrimination. Eventually, from the loss of discrimination, he perishes.

Don't we see the disastrous effect of the senses (greed, lust, material pursuits, crime, killing and others) on different people in today's world? This verse is so pragmatic in revealing the inner nature of man. So, Lord Krishna's advice is most relevant for all of us.

Verse 2-64

रागद्वेषवियुक्तैस्तु विषयानिन्द्रियैश्चरन् ।
आत्मवश्यैर्विधेयात्मा प्रसादमधिगच्छति ॥ २-६४॥

 Raagadwesha viyuktaistu vishayaan indriyaishcharan;
Aatmavashyair vidheyaatmaa prasaadam adhigacchati. 2-64

Explanation to Verse 2-64

रागद्वेषवियुक्तैः = रागश्च द्वेषश्च वियुक्तैः – free from attachment (attraction) and hate (repulsion), तु – but, विषयान्- sense objects इन्द्रियैः – by the senses, चरन् – moving, आत्मवश्यैः- under self-restraint, विधेयात्मा – the self-controlled man, प्रसादम् – Lord's mercy, peace, अधिगच्छति - attains

But the self-controlled man, moving amongst objects with the senses under restraint, and free from attraction and repulsion, attains peace.2-64

Commentary 2-64

Objects that are pleasing to the senses will always be there. They are external to us and one has little control on them. We must live in the midst of these objects. Stressing the importance of controlling the senses, Krishna describes a yogi as one who, despite moving amidst the sense objects, has control on his senses. He is free from likes and dislikes (*raaga dwesha viyuktaha*) and attains tranquility.

Verse 2-65

प्रसादे सर्वदुःखानां हानिरस्योपजायते ।

प्रसन्नचेतसो ह्याशु बुद्धिः पर्यवतिष्ठते ॥ २-६५॥

Prasaade sarvaduhkhaanaam haanir asyopajaayate;

Prasannachetaso hyaashu buddhih paryavatishthate. 2-65

Explanation to Verse 2-65

प्रसादे – in that peace (mercy of the Lord), सर्वदुःखानां – all pains हानिः – destruction, अस्य – his, उपजायते- arises प्रसन्नचेतसः – happy-minded, tranquil, हि – for, because आशु – very soon, बुद्धिः – intellect पर्यवतिष्ठते - परि + अव + तिष्ठते- well-established, steady

In that peace all pains are destroyed, for the intellect of the tranquil minded soon becomes steady 2-65

Commentary 2-65

In such a person who has attained tranquility, all his sorrows get destroyed. How? Because the intellect of this tranquil-minded person becomes firm and remains steady. Ehen the mind gets purified with control of the senses; all the internal disturbances cease to exist. It gets filled with joy, not from external sources but from oneself.

Verse 2-66

नास्ति बुद्धिरयुक्तस्य न चायुक्तस्य भावना ।

न चाभावयतः शान्तिरशान्तस्य कुतः सुखम् ॥ २-६६ ॥

Naasti buddhir ayuktasya na chaayuktasya bhaavanaa;

Na chaabhaavayatah shaantir ashaantasya kutah sukham 2-66

Explanation to Verse 2-66

नास्ति = न अस्ति, not is, बुद्धिरयुक्तस्य = बुद्धिः अयुक्तस्य, knowledge of the unsteady, न चायुक्तस्य = न not, च and अयुक्तस्य – of the unsteady, भावना – meditation न चाभावयतः = न not च and अभावयतः unmeditative शान्तिरशान्तस्य = शान्तिः अशान्तस्य – peace and of the peaceless कुतः – where is, सुखम् - happiness

There is no knowledge of the Self to the unsteady, and to the unsteady no meditation is possible; and to the un-meditative there can be no peace; and to the man who has no peace, how can there be happiness? 2-66

Commentary 2-66

Highlighting the importance of sense and mind control, Lord Krishna says that wisdom does not come to the fickle-minded. Yoga is the science of self-control – not merely a set of physical exercises as mostly done in the Western world!

Patanjali's yoga sastra focuses more on the mind than the body. For a person who does not practice self-discipline, meditation is not possible. To him, there is no peace. How can a person be happy without peace of mind? Practice alone makes a person perfect!

Verse 2-67

इन्द्रियाणां हि चरतां यन्मनोऽनुविधीयते ।

तदस्य हरति प्रज्ञां वायुर्नावमिवाम्भसि ॥ २-६७॥

 Indriyaanaam hi charataam yanmano'nuvidheeyate;

Tadasya harati prajnaam vaayur naavam ivaambhasi.2-67

Explanation to Verse 2-67

इन्द्रियाणां – of the senses, हि –for, चरतां – wandering, यन्मनोऽनुविधीयते = यत् which, मनः mind, अनुविधीयते follows, तदस्य = तत् – that अस्य his, हरति – carries away, प्रज्ञां – intelligence, power of discrimination वायुर्नावमिवाम्भसि= वायुः – wind + नावम् – boat + इव – like + अम्भसि – on the water

For the mind which follows in the wake of the wandering senses, carries away his discrimination as the wind (carries away) a boat on the water.2-67

Commentary 2-67

What happens to a person without discipline of mind? Lord Krishna provides an example here. Just as a strong wind (storm or gale) pushes away a boat on the waters, the mind that yields to the wandering senses carries away the wisdom of the person. A boat has very little control over a storm and loses its steering power. Likewise, the undisciplined mind has no control over the senses and loses its power of discrimination.

Verse 2-68

तस्माद्यस्य महाबाहो निगृहीतानि सर्वशः ।

इन्द्रियाणीन्द्रियार्थेभ्यस्तस्य प्रज्ञा प्रतिष्ठिता ॥ २-६८॥

Tasmaad yasya mahaabaaho nigriheetaani sarvashah;

Indriyaanee indriyaarthebhyas tasya prajnaa pratishthitaa 2-68

Explanation to Verse 2-68

तस्मात् - therefore, यस्य – whose, महाबाहो – mighty-armed, निगृहीतानि – restrained, सर्वशः   all-round, completely, इन्द्रियाणि -the senses, इन्द्रियार्थेभ्यः from the sense objects, तस्य – his ,प्रज्ञा – knowledge, प्रतिष्ठिता - is fixed, steady

Therefore, O mighty-armed Arjuna, his knowledge is steady whose senses are completely restrained from sense-objects! 2-68

Commentary 2-68

This verse concludes the topic on the qualities of *'sthitha pragjyah'* – a man of steady mind. Addressing Arjuna as *'mahaabaaho'* - the mighty-armed, Lord Krishna tells him that from the foregoing, please understand that the knowledge of the person whose sense organs are completely restrained from sense objects becomes firm.

Verse 2-69

या निशा सर्वभूतानां तस्यां जागर्ति संयमी ।

यस्यां जाग्रति भूतानि सा निशा पश्यतो मुनेः ॥ २-६९॥

Yaanishaa sarvabhootaanaam tasyaam jaagarti samyamee;

Yasyaam jaagrati bhootaani saa nishaa pashyato muneh. 2-69

Explanation to Verse 2-69

या - which निशा – night, सर्वभूतानां – to all beings, तस्यां - in that, जागर्ति – is awake, संयमी – the self-controlled,यस्यां – in which, जाग्रति – are awake, भूतानि – all beings, सा – that is, निशा – night, पश्यतो – who sees (introspects), मुनेः for the sage

That which is night to all beings, then the self-controlled man is awake; when all beings are awake, that is night for the sage who sees. 2-69

Commentary 2-69

What kind of transformation takes place in a man who can control his senses completely? There is an answer contained in this verse. It throws light on a unique quality of the wise. The people who are bound by the senses get immersed in mundane things in life. However, a jnani, the wise sage looks at things in a totally different perspective.

The Muni (sage) wise does not view the differences the way ordinary people see. He sees divinity (*brahmam*) in everything. For him, the night to all beings, is wakeful day; and the day when all beings are awake, is night. The Muni looks at things in the way of *advaitam* – no two entities.

Verse 2-70

आपूर्यमाणमचलप्रतिष्ठं समुद्रमापः प्रविशन्ति यद्वत् ।

तद्वत्कामा यं प्रवशिन्ति सर्व स शान्तिमाप्नोति न कामकामी ॥ २-७० ॥

Aapooryamaanam achalapratishtham Samudram aapah

pravishanti yadwat;

Tadwat kaamaa yam pravishanti sarve Sa shaantim aapnoti na kaamakaami. 2-70

Explanation to Verse 2-70

आपूर्यमाणम् - filled from all sides, अचलप्रतिष्ठम् – firmly fixed, समुद्रम् ocean, आपः – waters, प्रविशन्ति – enters, यद्वत् – as, तद्वत् so, कामाः – desires, यं –whom, प्रविशन्ति – enters, सर्वे – all, सः – he, शान्तिम्- peace आप्नोति – attains, न – not, कामकामी – full of desires

He attains peace into whom all desires enter as waters enter the ocean, which, filled from all sides, remains unmoved; but not the man who is full of desires.2-70

Commentary 2-70

A nice example is provided by Lord Krishna to help people understand the earlier verse. The huge ocean is already full, and it remains unaffected by the waters entering it. Likewise, the jnani's mind is always full and he is not impacted by the entry of sense objects in his mind. He enjoys absolute peace without desiring any sense objects.

Verse 2-71

विहाय कामान्यः सर्वान्पुमांश्चरति निःस्पृहः ।

निर्ममो निरहङ्कारः स शान्तिमधिगच्छति ॥ २-७१ ॥

Vihaaya kaamaan yah sarvaan pumaamshcharati nihsprihah;
Nirmamo nirahankaarah sa shaantim adhigacchati. 2-71

Explanation to Verse 2-71

विहाय – abandoning, कामान् – desires, यः – that, सर्वान्- all, पुमान्- man, चरति -moves, निःस्पृहः –without longing, निर्ममः –without a sense of ownership, निरहंकारः:- without egoism, सः – he, शान्तिम् – peace, अधिगच्छति - attains

The man attains peace, who, abandoning all desires, moves about without longing, without the sense of mine and without egoism.2-71

Commentary 2-71

The jnani's state of mind is such that it is not influenced by any sense objects. Such a wise person who lives without any longing (*nihsprhah*), freed from all desires, and without having any egoistic feelings of "I" and "Mine," (*nirmamao, nirahankaraha)* attains peace. He enjoys life with peace.

Verse 2-72

एषा ब्राह्मी स्थितिः पार्थं नैनां प्राप्य विमुह्यति ।

स्थित्वास्यामन्तकालेऽपि ब्रह्मनिर्वाणमृच्छति ॥२-७२॥

Eshaa braahmee sthitih paartha nainaam praapya vimuhyati;
Sthitwa asyaa mantakaale'pi brahma nirvana mricchati. 2-72

Explanation to Verse 2-72

एषा – this, ब्राह्मी- of Brahman, स्थितिः – state. पार्थं, O'Arjuna, न - not, एनां – this, प्राप्य-having obtained, विमुह्यति – is deluded. स्थित्वा - being established, अस्याम् - in this, अन्तकाले – at the end of life, अपि – even, ब्रह्मनिर्वाणम् – oneness with Brahman, ऋच्छति- attains

This is the Brahmic seat (eternal state), O son of Pritha! Attaining this, none is bewildered. Being established in it, even at the time of death, one attains oneness with Brahman 2-72

Commentary 2-72

Lord Krishna goes on to define the state of mind described in the earlier verse. O'Arjuna (Partha), This state is called *"Brahmi Sthitih"* – the state of Brahman. It is attained by a thorough knowledge of the Self. None who attains this state gets bewildered by the conflicts in life. Attaining it even towards the end of one's life, a man unites with the Brahman.

4.1 Conclusion of Chapter 2

ॐ तत्सदिति श्रीमद्भगवद्गीतासूपनिषत्सु

ब्रह्मविद्यायां योगशास्त्रे श्रीकृष्णार्जुनसंवादे

साङ्ख्ययोगो नाम द्वितीयोऽध्यायः ॥ २॥

Hari Om!

Om tatsad iti srimad bhagavad gitasupanisatsu brahmavidyaayaam yoga sastre sri Krishnarjunasamvaade saamkhya yogo naama dviteeyodhyaayah ll

Thus, in the Upanishad of the Bhagavad Gita, the knowledge of the Brahman, the science of Yoga, and the dialogue between Sri Krishna and Arjuna, ends the second discourse entitled Samkhya Yoga.

5 Srimad Bhagavad Gita Chapter 3- Karmayoga

The Yoga of Action

अथ तृतीयोऽध्यायः । कर्मयोगः ।

Chapter 3 has 43 Shlokas

The first two verses: Arjuna is confused. what path to follow – *Jnana* Knowledge or *Karma* Action. Questions Lord Krishna replies – setting the foundation for this Chapter 3.

Verse 3.1

अर्जुन उवाच ।

ज्यायसी चेत्कर्मणस्ते मता बुद्धिर्जनार्दन ।

तत्किं कर्मणि घोरे मां नियोजयसि केशव ॥ ३-१ ॥

Arjuna Uvaacha

Jyaayasee chet karmanaste mataa buddhir janaardana;

Tat kim karmani ghore maam niyojayasi keshava 3.1

Explanation to Verse 3.1

अर्जुन उवाच – Arjuna said, ज्यायसी – (ज्या-to grow old, ज्येष्ठ-senior) –better (comp)चेत्कर्मणस्ते मता बुद्धिर्जनार्दन= चेत् कर्मणः (अस्ति) ते मता बुद्धिः जनार्दन - If, in your opinion, intellect is better than performing duty, तत्किं कर्मणि घोरे मां

नियोजयसि केशव = तत् किं मां घोरे (R घुर् - Terrible, Cry) ,कर्मणि नियोजयसि (Rनि-युज) – Then, Keshava, why do you engage me in this terrible action?

O Janardhana, if you think that knowledge is superior to action, O Keshava, why then, you ask me to engage in this terrible action? 3.1

Commentary 3.1

After listening to Lord Krishna's advice in Chapter 2, Arjuna responds with a question. Clearly, Arjuna is confused by Jnanam (Knowledge) and Karma (Action). The Lord had talked about both knowledge and action by explaining the supremacy of a jnani (the enlightened) and highlighting the importance of Karma in verses 2.47 and 2.48. Arjuna compares both these paths and asks Lord Krishna that if Jnanam is superior to Karma, then why should he be engaged in this terrible warfare (which is full of action).

MESSAGE: This verse is an example to show that questioning is permitted in Sanaatana Dharma. Many Upanishads have been written based on questions.

Verse 3.2

व्यामिश्रेणेव वाक्येन बुद्धिं मोहयसीव मे ।

तदेकं वद निश्चित्य येन श्रेयोऽहमाप्नुयाम् ॥ ३-२॥

Vyaamishreneva vaakyena buddhim mohayaseeva me;

Tadekam vada nishchitya yena shreyo'ham aapnuyaam 3-2

Explanation to Verse 3.2

व्यामिश्रेणेव = व्यामिश्रेण इव - व्यामिश्र - mingled, not clear, equivocal, वाक्येन -words बुद्धिं - intellect मोहयसीव = मोहयसि इव (Rमुह्) –bewilder, confuse मे -me तदेकं - तत् एकं – therefore, only one वद – tell निश्चित्य = R(निश्) चित् -certain understanding - येन श्रेयोऽहमाप्नुयाम् = श्रेयः(Rश्रि) अहम् आप्नुयाम् - by which I may attain bliss

My intellect is confused with these mingled words; therefore, tell me that only certain way by which I may attain bliss.

Commentary 3-2

Arjuna continues to express his confusion caused by the seemingly conflicting statements by Lord Krishna. He thinks that he has an option to choose one of the paths – either Jnana or Karma. He pleads with Krishna to clarify which path is definitely superior to enable him to follow that path to attain the supreme. Lord Krishna provides the answer in the following verses.

Verse 3-3

श्रीभगवानुवाच ।

लोकेऽस्मिन् द्विविधा निष्ठा पुरा प्रोक्ता मयानघ ।

ज्ञानयोगेन साङ्ख्यानां कर्मयोगेन योगिनाम् ॥ ३-३ ॥

Sri Bhagavaan Uvaacha:

Loke'smin dwividhaa nishthaa puraa proktaa mayaanagha;

Jnaanayogena saankhyaanaam karmayogena yoginaam.3-3

Explanation to Verse 3-3

श्रीभगवानुवाच । Shri Bhagavan said लोकेऽस्मिन् - In this world, द्वि-विधा – two kinds of निष्ठा – नि-स्था – (placed in) faith पुरा – earlier प्रोक्ता - said मया – by me, अनघ – अन + अघ - Sinless one, ज्ञानयोगेन – linking the path of knowledge साङ्ख्यानां –of the philosophers कर्मयोगेन- by linking the process of action योगिनाम् –of the yogis ॥ ३-३ ॥

In this world there is a twofold path, as I said before, O sinless one, —the path of knowledge of the Sankhyas and the path of action of the Yogis! 3.3

Commentary 3.3

Lord Krishna addresses Arjuna as *'Anagha'* – O' Sinless one! Agam is sin and Anagah is sinless. In Sanskrit, the addition of 'A' as a prefix usually means the opposite. For example, Nyaya and Anyaya, Krama and Akrama, Eka and Aneka. So easy and nice.

Krishna points out that in this world there are two paths to attain immortality, as said by Him before *(maya prokta)*, — the path of knowledge of the Saankhyas and the path of action of the Yogis!

Verse 3-4

न कर्मणामनारम्भान्नैष्कर्म्यं पुरुषोऽश्नुते ।

न च संन्यसनादेव सिद्धिं समधिगच्छति ॥ ३-४॥

Na karmanaam anaarambhaan naishkarmyam purusho'shnute;
Na cha sannyasanaad eva siddhim samadhigacchati 3-4

Explanation to Verse 3-4

न कर्मणाम - of actions/duties नारम्भा = अन्-आरम्भात् – by non-performance नैष्कर्म्यं – actionless पुरुषोऽश्नुते = पुरुषः न अश्नुते – a man does not achieve न च – nor also संन्यसनादेव = संन्यसनात् एव –by renunciation, सिद्धिं – success/perfection समधिगच्छति = सम्-अधिगच्छति - attains

A man does not reach actionlessness by the non-performance of actions, nor does he attain to perfection by mere renunciation

Commentary 3.4

In Sanyasa Suktham, there is a line that reads: *'Na karmana na prajaya dhanena tyage naike amritatva manashuh.'* It means that

'Neither by rituals, nor by progeny nor by riches but by renunciation alone one can attain immortality.'

Purusha Suktham too says, *"Tamevam vidvan amrita iha bhavati nanyah pantha ayanaya vidyate"* meaning, 'For attaining liberation there is no other path (than knowledge of this Purusha, the Supreme Lord).

So, many scriptures point out that the nectar of liberation can be achieved only by jnana yoga but one must go through the Karma Yoga first.

In this verse, Lord Krishna emphasizes the importance of karma. How? He says, Arjuna, you should not avoid action (karma). Why? You cannot get peace of mind by running away from your duty. A diamond gets a shine only after grinding and polishing. Gold shines only after it goes through the melting and other processes. By giving up action, you cannot get moksha or liberation.

In the second line, Lord Krishna says *'sannyaasanaadeva'* - by mere renunciation, *siddhim na samadhigacchati* – a person can never acquire siddhi (moksha or liberation) here. So, Sanyaasa alone (Eva is important word – alone) does not guarantee Moksha. So, what gives Moksha? Sanyasa backed by Knowledge. One must be ripe with experience.

Verse 3-5

न हि कश्चित्क्षणमपि जातु तिष्ठत्यकर्मकृत् ।
कार्यते ह्यवशः कर्म सर्वः प्रकृतिजैर्गुणैः ॥ ३-५॥

Na hi kashchit kshanamapi jaatu tishthatyakarmakrit;
Kaaryate hyavashah karma sarvah prakritijair gunaih. 3-5

Explanation to Verse 3-5

हि – None indeed न कश्चित्क्षणमपि = न कश्चित् – none क्षणम् अपि - even for a moment अ-कर्म-कृत् – without action, न हि तिष्ठति – can ever remain हि –because सर्वः everyone ह्यवशः –helplessly कार्यते कर्म – made to perform action प्रकृतिजैर्गुणैः = प्रकृति-जैः गुणैः कार्यते - by the gunas born of prakrti.

Indeed, no one can ever remain without action even for a moment, because everyone is helplessly made to do action by the gunas born of prakriti.3.5

Commentary 3.5

However, giving up action completely is impossible, because everybody is forced to do some action or the other, governed by his basic traits -prakritir gunaih – the three gunas of prakṛti. So prakṛti means maaya, which is the basic cause of the creation; prakṛti or maaya is the basic cause of the creation; and this maaya is said to have three gunas – Satva, Rajas and Tamas – all three may exist in different proportions in people. There are tendencies inherited from parents. Like a monkey, mind keeps on jumping. Mind also cannot stop, because mind is not meant for stopping. Mind is meant for functioning. Therefore, vedantic meditation is not shutting down the complete thought process; not stilling the mind; but directing the mind; So, our aim should be not in stopping all actions but channelizing it – even in meditation.

Verse 3-6

कर्मेन्द्रियाणि संयम्य य आस्ते मनसा स्मरन् ।

इन्द्रियार्थान्विमूढात्मा मिथ्याचारः स उच्यते ॥ ३-६ ॥

Karmendriyaani samyamya ya aaste manasaa smaran;

Indriyaarthaan vimoodhaatmaa mithyaachaarah sa uchyate 3-6

Explanation to Verse 3-6

कर्मेन्द्रियाणि = कर्म-इन्द्रियाणि – the sense organs of action संयम्य – having restrained स न्विमूढात्मा = सः विमूढ-आत्मा – that deluded person, य आस्ते – who remains मनसा स्मरन् इन्द्रियार्थां = मनसा इन्द्रिय-अर्थान् स्मरन् – thinking of sense objects मिथ्याचारः = मिथ्या-आचारः – hypocrite, उच्यते-is called

Having restrained the sense organs of action, that deluded person who remains thinking on the sense-objects in his mind is called a hypocrite.3.6

Commentary 3.6

If the mind is not ripe for renunciation (sanyasam), one can become a pretender, a hypocrite having a double life like a split personality. Thus, in the last two verses (3.4, 3.5) and in this verse, Krishna provides the following three reasons on why Arjuna should pursue Karma Yoga first:

By avoiding Karma, you are not guaranteed liberation

Not doing any action or Karma is impossible because of inherent human tendencies (svabhaavam- traits of three gunas)

Suppressing desires and pretending to adopt inaction or renunciation is highly risky as mind tends to wander.

Verse 3-7

यस्त्विन्द्रियाणि मनसा नियम्यारभतेऽर्जुन ।
कर्मेन्द्रियैः कर्मयोगमसक्तः स विशिष्यते ॥ ३-७॥

Yastwindriyaani manasaa niyamyaarabhate'rjuna;
Karmendriyaih karmayogam asaktah sa vishishyate 3-7

Explanation to Verse 3-7

अर्जुनः O Arjuna तु –but इन्द्रियाणि – sense organs (of knowledge) मनसा by the mind नियम्य restrained कर्म-इन्द्रियैः -sense organs of action कर्म-योगम् – karma yoga असक्तः without attachment आरभते –begins सः he विशिष्यते - is far better, excels

Oh Arjuna! But, having restrained the organs of knowledge by the mind, he who pursues karmayōga with the organs of action without attachment is by far better. 3.7

Commentary 3.7

In Sanatana Dharma, there are four important pursuits in a person's life. They are described as: *Dharma, Artha, Kaama, and Moksham.* These include righteous living, material pursuits, desires, and eventually liberation respectively. Leading a clean dharmic (righteous) life in society, doing good to self and others through ethical means are prescribed in the Sastras. So, there is plenty of scope for fulfilling one's desires at the same time be useful to society. It is an ideal way to pursue Karma Yoga.

A householder *(grihasthaa)* is given freedom to fulfil his materialistic and personal desires like money, possessions, family, house, status, name, fame, and others (kaama, artha). However, he needs to regulate his sense organs, and not allow them to roam freely. Having controlled his senses, the person who pursues karma yoga without attachment excels even a sanyasi who is immature.

Verse 3-8

नियतं कुरु कर्म त्वं कर्म ज्यायो ह्यकर्मणः ।
शरीरयात्रापि च ते न प्रसिध्येदकर्मणः ॥ ३-८॥

Niyatam kuru karma twam karma jyaayo hyakarmanah;
Shareerayaatraapi cha te na prasiddhyed akarmanah. 3-8

Explanation to Verse 3-8

नियतं – binding, restraining कुरु – perform, कर्म – duty, त्वं – your कर्म – action ज्यायो – superior, ह्यकर्मणः = हि + अ-कर्मणः – for, because + inaction च – and शरीरयात्रापि = शरीर-यात्रा अपि – body maintenance even, ते – your, न प्रसिध्येदकर्मणः = न प्रसिध्येत् अ-कर्मणः – not possible by inaction

Perform your bounden duty, for action is superior to inaction and even the maintenance of the body would not be possible for you by inaction 3-8

Commentary 3-8

The importance of performing obligatory rituals is stressed in this verse. It is the starting point of Karma Yoga. None needs to give up legitimate pursuits necessary for livelihood. But, while being so engaged, we should not lose sight of the essential purpose of life. We have installations. We should constantly endeavor to purify our thoughts and speech and seek the grace of the Divine Mother, by which alone one can get the strength to control *kaama* and *krodha*.

A dancer balancing a pot on her head, while going through the various movements of the hands and the feet to the accompaniment of music, never for once forgets the pot on the head. Similarly, we should not lose sight of the purpose of life while engaged in our day-to-day activities.

Verse 3-9

यज्ञार्थात्कर्मणोऽन्यत्र लोकोऽयं कर्मबन्धनः ।
तदर्थं कर्म कौन्तेय मुक्तसङ्गः समाचर ॥ ३-९ ॥

Yajnaarthaat karmano'nyatra loko'yam karmabandhanah;

Tadartham karma kaunteya muktasangah samaachara. 3-9

Explanation to Verse 3-9

यज्ञार्थात्कर्मणोऽन्यत्र = यज्ञ-अर्थात्, कर्मणः अन्यत्र – for the sake of sacrifice, actions otherwise, लोकोऽयं कर्मबन्धनः = अयम् लोकः कर्म-बन्धनः – this world, bound by action, तदर्थं तत्-अर्थम् – for that sake कर्म – action कौन्तेय – O Son of Kunti मुक्तसङ्गः मुक्त-सङ्गः – free from attachment समाचर-सम्-आचर - perform

The world is bound by actions other than those performed for the sake of sacrifice; do, therefore, O son of Kunti, perform action for that sake (for sacrifice) alone, free from attachment!3-9

Commentary 3-9

Arjuna is addressed here as Kaunteya - O son of Kunti. Yagna is considered as duty with devotion. Action should be viewed as worship - not as a bondage!

Nowaday, life style of most individuals such a stress that actions are viewed as burdens; so many people are talking about stress management; Imagine offering your action or work as an expression of gratitude towards the Lord; an expression of gratitude out of love for Him for having provided you with five senses to enjoy life, the five elements from which you get all products for your life. There is an adage "Work is Worship." If such an attitude of looking at work as an offering to the Almighty is adopted, stress will vanish. You will be able to lead life with a new outlook and renewed vigor. Otherwise, work will feel like a burden. Treating work as Yagna leads to peace. This is a secret of Karma Yoga. In the following verse, Lord Krishna presents in Karma Yoga in different perspectives.

Verse 3-10

सहयज्ञाः प्रजाः सृष्ट्वा पुरोवाच प्रजापतिः ।

अनेन प्रसविष्यध्वमेष वोऽस्त्विष्टकामधुक् ॥ ३-१० ॥

Sahayajnaah prajaah srishtwaa, purovaacha prajaapatih;

Anena prasa vishyadhwamesha, vo'stvishta kaamadhuk. 3-10

Explanation to Verse 3-10

सहयज्ञाः प्रजाः सृष्ट्वा पुरोवाच प्रजापतिः = पुरा – in the beginning, प्रजापतिः – Brahma – the Creator, सृष्ट्वा – having created प्रजाः – mankind, सहयज्ञाः – together with sacrifice, उवाच – said, अनेन – by this, प्रसविष्यध्वमेष- प्रसविष्यध्वम् एषः – you shall propagate, this, वोऽस्त्विष्टकामधुक् = वः –your इष्ट- desires काम-धुक् – Kamadhenu (mythological milch cow), अस्तु – let it be.

The Creator, having in the beginning of creation created mankind together with sacrifice, said: "By this shall you propagate; let this be the milch cow of your desires (the cow which yields the desired objects)".

Commentary 3-10

Pura means long ago. According to the Vedas, Lord Brahma, the supreme creator, created all the living beings, including the human beings. Thus, having created mankind, Lord Brahma (Prajapati) provided the Vedas for the benefit of human beings who are endowed with intelligence and the power of thinking. The Vedas are intended to be used as tools to lead a life of peace and harmony. Kaamadhuk mentioned here refers to the divine Kaamadhenu- the celestial cow that is believed to give whatever one needs. Vedas are not against material prosperity as they recommend pursuit of 'Dharma, Artha, Kaama and Moksha.' The Vedas, like Kaamadhenu, provide everything that a human being needs.

Verse 3-11

देवान्भावयतानेन ते देवा भावयन्तु वः ।
परस्परं भावयन्तः श्रेयः परमवाप्स्यथ ॥ ३-११॥

Devaan bhaavayataanena te devaa bhaavayantu vah;
Parasparam bhaavayantah shreyah param avaapsyatha. 3-11

Explanation to Verse 3-11

देवान् - अनेन -भावयत – The gods, with this, (you) nourish ते देवाः- भावयन्तु - वः - Those gods nourish you परस्परम् भावयन्तः – one another nourishing परम् -श्रेयः -अवाप्स्यथ – the highest, good (you) shall get

With this you nourish the gods, and may the gods nourish you; thus nourishing one another, you shall attain to the highest good.3-11

Commentary 3-11

How can we get all that we desire? This verse addresses this question. Let's ask - Who are the agents helping humanity? The five elements – air, water, fire, space and earth. There are the presiding deities (Devas) for each of these natural elements - the *Panchabhutas*. Indra - the lord of thunder and rain. Varuna- the lord of oceans. Agni – the Lord of fire and so on. If people need rain, they pray to Lord Varuna. By praying, you show your gratitude to them. In return, they will shower you with gifts. Instead, if we keep chopping down all the trees, it will have an impact on rainfall. Cosmic forces are Devas. Propitiate the Devas and you will reap rewards.

Verse 3-12

इष्टान्भोगान्हि वो देवा दास्यन्ते यज्ञभाविताः ।
तैर्दत्तानप्रदायैभ्यो यो भुङ्क्ते स्तेन एव सः ॥ ३-१२॥

Ishtaan bhogaan hi vo devaa daasyante yajnabhaavitaah;

Tair dattaan apradaayaibhyo yo bhungkte stena eva sah. 3-12

Explanation to Verse 3-12

इष्टान्भोगान्हि = इष्टान् भोगान् हि desired, objects, so वो देवा दास्यन्ते – the gods will give you यज्ञ-भाविताः - nourished by the sacrifice तैर्दत्तानप्रदायैभ्यो = तैः दत्तान् अ-प्रदाय एभ्यः – By them, given, without offering भुङ्क्ते – enjoys सः –he स्तेनः-thief एव -verily

The gods, nourished by the sacrifice, will give you the desired objects. So, he who enjoys the objects given by the gods without offering (in return) to them, is verily a thief.3-12

Commentary 3-12

Some people may not really care about the five elements and what is said in the previous verse. How are such people viewed? This verse gives the comment. Cherished by yagnas (offerings), the Devas bestow gifts for the humanity. Many yagnas are conducted even today for the benefit of humanity. We ought to feel indebted for what Mother Nature has provided us. Nothing is made in this world without the resources from Mother Nature.

Karma Yoga recommends performing Yajnas to seek benefits from Mother Nature. One who enjoys what is given by Nature without gratitude and not giving back anything is viewed as a thief who (mis) appropriates nature's free offerings. Destroying nature's gift mindlessly without offering anything in return by way of protecting them is criticized in this verse.

Verse 3-13

यज्ञशिष्टाशिनः सन्तो मुच्यन्ते सर्वकिल्बिषैः ।

भुञ्जते ते त्वघं पापा ये पचन्त्यात्मकारणात् ॥ ३-१३॥

Yajna shishtaashinah santo, muchyante sarva kilbishaih;

Bhunjate te twagham paapaa ye pachantyaatma kaaranaat. 3-13

Explanation to Verse 3-13

यज्ञशिष्टाशिनः = यज्ञ-शिष्ट-अशिनः, who eat of the remnants of the sacrifice सन्तः- the righteous, मुच्यन्ते – freed from सर्व-किल्बिषैः from all sins भुञ्जते -eat ते त्वघं – ते, तु -अघम् - those, indeed, sin ये पापाः those sinners, आत्म-कारणात् पचन्ति – for their own sake cook

The righteous, who eat of the remnants of the sacrifice, are freed from all sins; but those sinful ones who cook food (only) for their own sake, verily eat sin.3-13

Commentary 3-13

There is a beautiful verse in Sanskrit.

परोपकाराय फलन्ति वृक्षाः परोपकाराय वहन्ति नद्यः ।

परोपकाराय दुहन्ति गावः परोपकारार्थम् इदं शरीरम् ॥

paropakārāya phalanti vrikṣaḥ paropakārāya dhūhanti gāvahaḥ paropakārāya vahanti nadhyaḥ paropakārārtham idaṃ śarīram

Trees bear fruit for the benefit of others, and rivers flow for the benefit of others. Cows milk this body for the benefit of others.

Why should trees give you fruits? They don't eat them. They provide the fruits for us. Nature gives us a message of using our body to do self-less work for the help others.

Follow karma yoga, do not be indifferent to nature and exploit the natural elements to feed your greed; ingratitude is the worst weakness of a human being. Even for small kindness, we say Thanks. Why not for big things? That is why we say prayers in gratitude before eating food.

The Vedas prescribe five different Yagnas – called *'Pancha Maha Yagnas'* to be performed every day. These are: Nitya Karma (daily obligations), Deva Yagna (the worship of deities), Rishi Yagna (the adoration of the wise), Pitru Yagna (reverence to parents), Nara Yagna (services to mankind), and Bhuta Yagna (reverence to all living beings).

Now, in this verse, the Lord has added a new dimension to Karma Yoga. He prescribes yagnas as a method of attaining inner purification – a spiritual advancement - like a detergent cleans your clothes. One who practices these yagnams becomes free from all the sins.

The verse contains a subtle criticism of those people who do not contribute anything to the world; the selfish people who cook only for themselves – meaning those who do not want to share anything with other people. Such people do not contribute anything for the benefit of communities; they are useless to the society and hence attract sins. Even a small contribution goes a long way to help the less privileged.

Verse 3-14

अन्नाद्भवन्ति भूतानि पर्जन्यादन्नसम्भवः ।

यज्ञाद्भवति पर्जन्यो यज्ञः कर्मसमुद्भवः ॥ ३-१४॥

Annaad bhavanti bhootaani parjanyaad anna sambhavah;

Yajnaad bhavati parjanyo yajnah karma samudbhavah.3-14

Explanation to Verse 3-14

अन्नाद्भवन्ति = अन्नात् भवन्ति – From food come forth भूतानि – beings पर्जन्यादन्नसम्भवः = पर्जन्यात् अन्न-संभवः From rain, food is produced. यज्ञात् भवति पर्जन्यः- from sacrifices arises rain यज्ञः कर्म-समुद्भवः – **sacrifice is born of karma (action)**

From food come forth beings, and from rain food is produced; from sacrifice arises rain, and sacrifice is born of action.3-14

Commentary 3-14

This verse illustrates the wheel of life and how it works. For example, none can order rain. It is a gift from the heavens. Manusmriti says - The offering given to the fire in the Yagna reaches the sun; The sun causes rain to be produced; from rain food; that reaches all creatures. How can we believe that the offering to fire reaches the Sun. They are like the waves from the TV studios or Cell phone towers that reach you unseen by anyone.

MESSAGE: Food is essential for life and rains are essential to grow food. Yagnas help to produce rainfalls that in turn helps to grow crops and food.

Verse 3-15

कर्म ब्रह्मोद्भवं विद्धि ब्रह्माक्षरसमुद्भवम् ।
तस्मात्सर्वगतं ब्रह्म नित्यं यज्ञे प्रतिष्ठितम् ॥ ३-१५॥

Karma brahmodbhavam viddhi brahmaakshara samudbhavam;
Tasmaat sarvagatam brahma nityam yajne
pratishthitam.3-15

Explanation to Verse 3-15

कर्म -action ब्रह्मोद्भवं- ब्रह्म-उद्भवम् - comes from Brahma विद्धि - know –ब्रह्म – Brahma अक्षर- imperishable समुद्भवम् rises from तस्मात् – therefore सर्वगतम् – the all pervading ब्रह्म –Brahma नित्यम् यज्ञे प्रतिष्ठितम् - ever established in sacrifice

Know thou that action comes from Brahma, and Brahma proceeds from the Imperishable. Therefore, the all-pervading (Brahma) ever rests in sacrifice.3-15

Commentary 3-15

Karma Brahmodbhavam Viddhi refers to the very ability to act is a gift from the creator. The manifestation of the creative urge is *Brahma Akshara Samudbhavam*. Brahma here refers to the Vedas and Aksharam is Ishwara – the almighty. *brahmaaksharasamudbhavam* means Veda has emanated from the Lord. So, the all-pervading Brahman is ever present in Yagna – '*Nityam Yagne Pratishtitam.*' The verse is intended to proclaim that vedic teachings prescribe yagnas and karma yoga has arisen from the Vedas.

What is the impact of not engaging in yagnas? The following verse replies.

Verse 3-16

एवं प्रवर्तितं चक्रं नानुवर्तयतीह यः ।

अघायुरिन्द्रियारामो मोघं पार्थ स जीवति ॥ ३-१६॥

Evam pravartitam chakram naanuvartayateeha yah;

Aghaayur indriyaaraamo mogham paartha sa jeevati.3-16

Explanation to Verse 3-16

एवं प्रवर्तितं चक्रं = यः इह एवं प्रवर्तितं चक्रं – Thus, set is the revolving wheel, नानुवर्तयतीह यः= न अनुवर्तयति – does not follow, who, अघायुरिन्द्रियारामो = अघ-आयुः इन्द्रिय-आरामः – living in sin, rejoicing in the senses सः मोघम् जीवति - he lives in vain, पार्थ O Arjuna

He who does not follow the wheel thus set revolving, who lives in sinful life, rejoicing in the senses, he lives in vain, O Arjuna! 3-16

Commentary 3-16

This great wheel of life is set in motion by the Almighty (Nature) - it is a natural law. Nature is impartial and has only its own laws. Fire burns anyone putting a finger into it. So, humans have understood its nature and tamed the mighty natural forces to their own advantage by using God-given intellect. So, the more we understand nature, the more we respect her laws, the more we gain for our welfare. The atom has tremendous power in it, but we must know how to use it for human welfare – not for destruction. Those who dare oppose it, disrespect it will be mercilessly destroyed.

Krishna cautions Arjuna. In this world, he, who does not follow the (cosmic) cycle which is initiated (by the Lord) in this manner, is a sinful and sensual (person). He lives in vain, Oh Arjuna!

Verse 3-17

यस्त्वात्मरतिरेव स्यादात्मतृप्तश्च मानवः ।

आत्मन्येव च सन्तुष्टस्तस्य कार्यं न विद्यते ॥ ३-१७॥

Yastwaatmaratir eva syaad aatmatriptashcha maanavah;

Aatmanyeva cha santushtas tasya kaaryam na vidyate.3-17

Explanation to Verse 3-17

यस्त्वात्मरतिरेव = यः तु आत्म-रतिः एव, who, but, rejoices in the self only, स्यादात्मतृप्तश्च = स्यात् आत्म-तृप्तः च - who is contented in the Self मानवः –the man आत्मन्येव च सन्तुष्टस्तस्य = आत्मनि एव सन्तुष्टः च तस्य who is happy in the self alone, his कार्यं न विद्यते – work is nothing to do (no obligation)

But for that man who rejoices only in the Self, who is satisfied in the Self, who is content in the Self alone, verily there is nothing to do.3-17

Commentary 3-17

The benefits of karma yoga are explained in this and the next verse.

If there is a man who loves the Self, who is happy and contented with the Self (alone), there is nothing to be accomplished for him.

How do we attain such a state? See a child sometime. How the child engages himself in his own world playing with toys, unmindful of the external world.

By following karma yoga, you get the benefit of purifying your mind and go to the next stage of spiritual advancement. First stage is called *pravṛtti;* fulfill your aspirations as well as contribute to social living. In this spiritual advancement, there are different stages, and man gradually grows beyond desires and becomes more interested in self-satisfaction instead of material desires. This is how he enters the next stage nivṛtti or withdrawal phase. From Karma yoga, one advances into Jnana yoga. The discovery of the complete self is facilitated by Jnana yoga.

This stage-wise advancement to ultimate self-realization is also supported by research in the western world. One example is that of Maslow's theory of hierarchy.

Verse 3-18

नैव तस्य कृतेनार्थो नाकृतेनेह कश्चन ।

न चास्य सर्वभूतेषु कश्चिदर्थव्यपाश्रयः ॥ ३-१८॥

Naiva tasya kritenaartho naakriteneha kashchana;

Na chaasya sarvabhooteshu kashchidartha vyapaashrayah.3-18

Explanation to Verse 3-18

नैव तस्य = न एव तस्य – not even, of him कृतेनार्थो = कृतेन न अर्थः – by actions done, no interest or meaning न अ-कृतेन (कश्चन अर्थः) – by actions not done न च अस्य सर्व-भूतेषु – and, nor does this person amongst all beings कश्चिदर्थव्यपाश्रयः = कश्चित्, अर्थ-व्यपाश्रयः - depend on any being for any object.

For him there is no interest whatsoever in what is done or what is not done; nor does he depend on any being for any object.3-18

Commentary 3-18

An enlightened person called a jnaani will enjoy activities and inaction too. Because through action he does not expect any result nor any benefit. Similarly, through inaction too he does not desire any result; So, neither he is dependent on action; nor is he dependent on inaction. That is total freedom from any kind of emotional attachment. It is the height of enlightenment – rare and most difficult achievement for an average person.

We hear about great gurus (jnaanis) like Adi Sankaracharya, Ramana Maharishi, Sadashiva Brahmendral, Sri Raghavendra, Sai Baba who had reached such high levels of emotional detachment and wisdom. So, it is possible for human beings to reach such high levels of emotional quotient (EQ).

From verse 8 to 18, Lord Krishna speaks about the importance of Karma Yoga.

In the next verse he sums it up neatly.

Verse 3-19

तस्मादसक्तः सततं कार्यं कर्म समाचर ।

असक्तो ह्याचरन्कर्म परमाप्नोति पूरुषः ॥ ३-१९॥

Tasmaad asaktah satatam kaaryam karma samaachara;
Asakto hyaacharan karma param aapnoti poorushah.3-19

Explanation to Verse 3-19

तस्मादसक्तः = तस्मात् अ-सक्तः – Therefore, without attachment, सततम् – always, कार्यम् – that which should be done कर्म सम्-आचर – perform the action असक्तो ह्याचरन्कर्म = अ-सक्तः हि आचरन् कर्म – for, by performing action without attachment, पूरुषः परम् आप्नोति - man reaches the Supreme

Therefore, without attachment, do thou always perform action which should be done; for, by performing action without attachment man reaches the Supreme. 3-19

Commentary 3-19

This verse is a short and quick advice from Lord Krishna in encouraging Arjuna to fight. Follow the recommended stages of karma yoga – do your assigned duty responsibly without attachment to results and thus purify your mind. Then follow jnana yoga to discover your Self and thus be totally free.

In short, it is the vedic life program that prescribes the four stages in a man's life - *brahmacharyam, gruhastrashram, vaanaprastham and sanyaasam.*

Verse 3-20

कर्मणैव हि संसिद्धिमास्थिता जनकादयः ।
लोकसङ्ग्रहमेवापि सम्पश्यन्कर्तुमर्हसि ॥ ३-२० ॥

 Karmanaiva hi samsiddhim aasthitaa janakaadayah;
Lokasangraham evaapi sampashyan kartum arhasi.3-20

Explanation to Verse 3-20

कर्मणैव= कर्मणा एव – by action, only हि –verily संसिद्धिमास्थिता = संसिद्धिम् आस्थिताः - perfection attained जनकादयः - जनक-आदयः - Janaka and others लोकसङ्ग्रहमेवापि = लोक-संग्रहम् एव अपि – protection of the people, only सम्पश्यन्कर्तुमर्हसि = सम्पश्यन् कर्तुम् अर्हसि - with a view, you should perform action

Janaka and others attained perfection verily by action only; even with a view to the protection of the masses thou should perform action.3-20

Commentary 3-20

In understanding any advice, an example always helps. Lord Krishna gives here an example of people who have attained liberation by following the norms of duty. He cites Janaka Maharaj (King), father of Sita Devi.

Even a grihasthaa (a householder) in grihasthashram can follow spirituality and attain liberation. If you live in a community, for the sake of the society, you must continue to follow dharma; you do not follow karma yoga just for your sake or for your benefit alone. You must do for the benefit of the society. Because you happen to be in the society, you must do that for the sake of the wellbeing of the society.

In ancient times, the learned Khsatriyas, like King Janaka and others (Kings Ajathachatru, Aswapathi) strove to attain liberation through action itself. The meaning is that they remained established in liberation while continuing to work in their assigned duties. So, it is possible to attain enlightenment while still following your duty.

Verse 3-21

यद्यदाचरति श्रेष्ठस्तत्तदेवेतरो जनः ।

स यत्प्रमाणं कुरुते लोकस्तदनुवर्तते ॥ ३-२१ ॥

Yadyad aacharati shreshthas tattadevetaro janah;

Sa yat pramaanam kurute lokas tad anuvartate.3-21

Explanation to Verse 3-21

यद्यद = यत् यत, whatever, आ चरति – he does श्रेष्ठः –a great man तत् तत् एव – that, that alone इतरः जनः –other people सः –he यत् –whatever प्रमाणम् – example, standard कुरुते –does लोकः – the world तत् अनुवर्तते –follows that

Whatever a great man does, that other men follow; whatever he sets up as the standard, the world follows that. 3-21

Commentary 3.21

There is a Sanskrit proverb that says – *Yatha Raaja, Thata Praja* meaning Just as the King, the subjects are. In other words, people follow the standards set by their leader. Children tend to follow the role model set by the parents.

If the leader is dishonest and corrupt, how do you expect the followers to be honest? Clearly good leadership starts from the top down. It is also applicable to modern corporations and other organizations. So, leaders have a great responsibility to their followers; they must be conversant and follow ethical, moral and spiritual codes for good governance.

Verse 3-22

न मे पार्थास्ति कर्तव्यं त्रिषु लोकेषु किञ्चन ।

नानवाप्तमवाप्तव्यं वर्त एव च कर्मणि ॥ ३-२२॥

Na me paarthaasti kartavyam trishu lokeshu kinchana;

Naanavaaptam avaaptavyam varta eva cha karmani.3-22

Explanation to Verse 3-22

न- nothing, मे -me पार्थ -O Arjuna अस्ति- is कर्तव्यम् – to be done त्रिषु लोकेषु -in the three worlds किञ्चन -anything न- not अन्-अवास्तम् –unattained वर्ते –I am engaged एव च -certainly, also कर्मणि -in action

There is nothing in the three worlds, O Arjuna, that should be done by Me, nor is there anything unattained (that needs to be attained); yet I engage Myself in action! 3-22

Commentary 3-22

Lord Krishna cites Himself as an example for even jnaanis to engage in action. As Mahavishnu's avatara (incarnation), He need not engage Himself on the Battlefield of Kurukshetra. He could have been sitting comfortably in his royal palace in vaikuntam. Yet, he chose to be a driver for Arjuna to help him fight against adharma (lack of righteousness). To fight against adharma, He killed his own Uncle Kamsa. So, even Gods have a duty to do and continue to perform actions. CEO of a company does not mean sitting in a luxurious office but getting down to right action.

Verse 3-23

यदि ह्यहं न वर्तेयं जातु कर्मण्यतन्द्रितः ।
मम वर्त्मानुवर्तन्ते मनुष्याः पार्थ सर्वशः ॥ ३-२३ ॥

Yadi hyaham na varteyam jaatu karmanyatandritah;
Mama vartmaanuvartante manushyaah paartha sarvashah.3-23

Explanation to Verse 3-23

यदि – if, हि –surely, अहम् –I, न वर्तेयम् –not engage in action, जातु-ever कर्मणि –in action, अतन्द्रितः – unwearied, मम –my वर्त्म – path अनुवर्तन्ते – follow, मनुष्याः –men, पार्थ –O Arjuna, सर्वशः in every way

For, should I not ever engage Myself in action, unwearied, men would in every way follow My path, O Arjuna!

Commentary 3-23

Gita continues to emphasize the importance of each one performing one's duty diligently. Krishna urges Arjuna to always perform action and not give in to the human tendency to become lazy, even if we can afford to be so. Krishna says whatever you do, do it wholeheartedly, with devotion and sincerity.

Peter F. Drucker, the management guru said, "There is an enormous number of managers who have retired on the job." We see that some people do not like to work. Some do grudgingly, with no real interest in the work.

Verse 3-24

उत्सीदेयुरिमे लोका न कुर्यां कर्म चेदहम् ।

सङ्करस्य च कर्ता स्यामुपहन्यामिमाः प्रजाः ॥ ३-२४॥

Utseedeyur ime lokaa na kuryaam karma ched aham;

Sankarasya cha kartaa syaam upahanyaam imaah prajaah.3-24

Explanation to Verse 3-24

उत्सीदेयुरिमे = उत्सीदेयुः इमे – would perish, these अहम्- I, कर्म न कुर्याम्(V) – did not perform action, चेत् –if, लोकाः (P) worlds (अहम) संकरस्य- confusion of castes, च - &,कर्ता author, स्यामुपहन्यामिमाः = स्याम् उपहन्याम् इमाः - would be, प्रजाः-beings

These worlds would perish if I did not perform action; I should be the author of confusion of castes and destruction of these beings 3-24

Commentary 3-24

If a person does not perform the assigned work, there is a risk of a backlash.

Lord Krishna cites Himself as an example saying, "If I do not do my duty and set myself as a role model, I will create confusion in the minds of people on their duties and thus, I will be destroying them."

There are many ways open to select one's profession. You can follow your family tradition, where your ancestors excelled - like a lawyer, doctor, soldier, sculptor, weaver – whatever, because the advantage is that you are exposed to it from your childhood and seen your father and grandfather at work. With modern technology, you improve on the techniques, but you do not go far away from the basic line of work of your ancestors Varna or profession.

Alternatively, you can follow your natural qualities, aptitudes or inclinations. Take up work that you really love, like being an engineer, electrical or mechanical whatever, artists, artisans, teachers – not the job that may pay you high but one that suits your natural taste and skills.

Verse 3-25

सक्ताः कर्मण्यविद्वांसो यथा कुर्वन्ति भारत ।

कुर्याद्विद्वांस्तथासक्तश्चिकीर्षुर्लोकसङ्ग्रहम् ॥ ३-२५॥

 Saktaah karmanyavidwaamso yathaa kurvanti bhaarata;

Kuryaad vidwaam stathaa saktash chikeershur lokasangraham.3-25

Explanation to Verse 3-25

सक्ताः - attached, कर्मण्यविद्वांसो = कर्मणि अ-विद्वांसः – to action, the ignorant, यथा – as,कुर्वन्ति- act, भारत – O Arjuna कुर्याद्विद्वांस्तथासक्तश्चिकीर्षुर्लोकसङ्ग्रहम् = कुर्यात्- विद्वान्- तथा (एव) - असक्तः – चिकीर्षुः- लोक-संग्रहम् Should act - wise- so- unattached- wishing- welfare of the world

As the ignorant men act from attachment to action, O Bharata (Arjuna), so should the wise act without attachment, wishing the welfare of the world!

Commentary 3-25

In this verse, there is a reference to the wise person (Jnaani) and an ignorant person (Ajnaani).

Just as the ignorant acts from attachment to action, the wise should act without attachment in the interest of the society at large. Though both act, the difference is in the attitude.

Verse 3-26

न बुद्धिभेदं जनयेदज्ञानां कर्मसङ्गिनाम् ।
जोषयेत्सर्वकर्माणि विद्वान्युक्तः समाचरन् ॥ ३-२६ ॥

 Na buddhibhedam janayed ajnaanaam
karmasanginaam;
Joshayet sarva karmaani vidwaan yuktah
samaacharan.3-26

Explanation to Verse 3-26

न-no, बुद्धिभेदं = बुद्धि-भेदम् – unsettlement in the mind, जनयेदज्ञानां = जनयेत् अज्ञानाम् – should produce of the ignorant, कर्म सङ्गिनाम् – who are attached to action, जोषयेत्सर्वकर्माणि = जोषयेत् सर्व-कर्माणि - should engage them in all actions विद्वान्युक्तः = विद्वान् युक्तः – the wise, engaged समाचरन् = सम्-आचरन् - performing

Let no wise man unsettle the minds of ignorant people who are attached to action; he should engage them in all actions, himself fulfilling them with devotion 3-26

Commentary 3-26

The word *'karmasangi'* refers to those people who are attached to worldly activities and their results mostly materialistic. This is the most common variety of people in today's world. We cannot ask them to give up all those activities, detract or confuse them with advice to give up materialism and become Sanyaasis and Jnaanis. Who wants it? Such philosophy of renunciation is given only to those in an acceptable state of mind. It is not for everybody.

Here is where Vedas shine. They provide the path of Dharma- Artha- Kaama - Moksham. The Vedas are not against pursuing legitimate pleasures. For every age, there is a prescribed path – to produce joy, you must give an appropriate toy to a child. They have ages marked on toy boxes.

The doctor gives different medicines for different people though the human body is the same. Homeopathy treats two people with same indications differently because of their different mind sets. So, if the wise dispenses a difficult philosophy to a karmasangi, it will not be effective. So, like in America there is an expression – let's make a deal- the wise make a deal with people – allow them to pursue their interests, but at the same time engage, persuade them by performing with involvement activities that appeal to them.

Verse 3-27

प्रकृतेः क्रियमाणानि गुणैः कर्माणि सर्वशः ।

अहङ्कारविमूढात्मा कर्ताहमिति मन्यते ॥ ३-२७॥

Prakriteh kriyamaanaani gunaih karmaani sarvashah;
Ahamkaaravimoodhaatmaa kartaaham iti manyate.3-27

Explanation to Verse 3-27

प्रकृतेः – of nature, क्रियमाणानि – done, performed गुणैः – by the qualities, कर्माणि – actions, सर्वशः-in all cases, अहङ्कार-विमूढ-आत्मा - one whose mind is deluded by egoism, अहम् – I, कर्ता – the doer इति –thus, मन्यते -thinks

Actions are performed in all cases by the qualities of Nature only. He whose mind is deluded by egoism thinks: "I am the doer". 3-27

Commentary 3-27

There is more philosophy in this verse. The body-mind-complex typically called *'ahamkara'* is Sanskrit refers to the arrogant, proud attitude or ego in the physical self. Everybody is a mixture of ahamkaara and aatma. Ahamkaara is called as Ego or the lower self, Atma is the higher Self.

The I is of two kinds – one that refers to ego; the mind in the physical self. The other refers to a higher plane of self – Atma or soul. When you say Aham Brahasmi – I am brahman – you refer to the big I. This verse talks about the lower I – the ignorant man who thinks that he is the doer – while he is driven by the three gunas of prakriti – *Sattva, Rajas and Tamas.* Often clouded by egoism of the lower self, man thinks. "I am the doer."

Verse 3-28

तत्त्ववित्तु महाबाहो गुणकर्मविभागयोः ।
गुणा गुणेषु वर्तन्त इति मत्वा न सज्जते ॥ ३-२८॥

Tattwavittu mahaabaaho gunakarma vibhaagayoh;
Gunaa guneshu vartanta iti matwaa na sajjate.3-28

Explanation to Verse 3-28

तत्त्व-वित् तु – the knower of the truth, महा-बाहो – mighty armed, गुण-कर्म-विभागयोः - the divisions of the qualities and their functions, गुणाः - the qualities, गुणेषु वर्तन्ते इति मत्वा न सज्जते

But he who knows the truth, O mighty-armed Arjuna, about the divisions of the qualities and their functions, knowing that the

Gunas as senses move amidst the Gunas as the sense-objects, is not attached.3-28

Commentary 3-28

What about the *Jnaani*- the wise or enlightened one? How is he different?

As we saw before, *ajnaani* (unwise) performs action for the sake of getting happiness, whereas a jnaani performs action with happiness seeking fulfilment. So, one performs for the sake of happiness, while the other performs with happiness.

You cannot escape from the miseries of the world. Only foolish people tired of the world take to drinks and drugs. Even that will not improve, as most of the time they are going to become more miserable and incapable of facing the world; therefore, better to accept the fact that you must face the world and interact with the world.

Many saints have demonstrated this difference. In ancient times and recent times. Purandaradasa, the father of Carntic music was a rich jeweler who became an enlightened saint. Pundalika became one in Pandharpur (Maharashtra). Ramana Maharishi, Kanchi Maha Periyava and many more have taught on the intricacies of dharmic living and attain happiness.

Verse 3-29

प्रकृतेर्गुणसम्मूढाः सज्जन्ते गुणकर्मसु ।
तानकृत्स्नविदो मन्दान्कृत्स्नविन्न विचालयेत् ॥ ३-२९॥

Prakriter gunasammoodhaah sajjante gunakarmasu;
Taan akritsnavido mandaan kritsnavin na vichaalayet.3-29

Explanation to Verse 3-29

प्रकृतेः – of nature, गुण-सम्मूढाः – deluded by the gunas, सज्जन्ते – are attached, गुण-कर्मसु – in the functions of the qualities, तान् – those, अ-कृत्स्न-विदः – of imperfect, knowledge मन्दान् – the foolish, कृत्स्न-वित् - man of knowledge, न विचालयेत - should not unsettle

Those deluded by the qualities of Nature are attached to the functions of the qualities. A man of perfect knowledge should not unsettle the foolish one of imperfect knowledge.3-29

Commentary 3-29

Discrimination between Atma and Parakriti can cause confusion. In a tender form, one cannot differentiate between the skin and the pulp. Only after the fruits becomes ripe, a distinct difference can about between the skin and the pulp.

Verse 3-30

मयि सर्वाणि कर्माणि संन्यस्याध्यात्मचेतसा ।

निराशीर्निर्ममो भूत्वा युध्यस्व विगतज्वरः ॥ ३-३० ॥

Mayi sarvaani karmaani sannyasyaadhya atmachetasaa;

Niraasheer nirmamo bhootwaa yudhyaswa vigatajwarah.3-30

Explanation to Verse 3-30

मयि – in me, सर्वाणि – all कर्माणि – actions संन्यस्याध्यात्मचेतसा = संन्यस्य –अध्य-आत्म -चेतसा –renouncing - with the mind centred in the Self, निराशीर्निर्ममो = निर्-आशीः - निर्-ममः – free from worry about results and egoism, भूत्वा –so being, युध्यस्व - fight, विगत-ज्वरः without mental fever(lethargy)

Renouncing all actions in Me, with the mind centred in the Self, free from desire and egoism, and without being lethargic, fight! 3-30

Commentary 3-30

This is an important verse. The Lord dispels Arjuna's mental fever by encouraging him to fight free from worry about the results. Put the burden on the Lord and act is the core meaning of this verse.

Verse 3-31

ये मे मतमिदं नित्यमनुतिष्ठन्ति मानवाः ।

श्रद्धावन्तोऽनसूयन्तो मुच्यन्ते तेऽपि कर्मभिः ॥ ३-३१ ॥

Ye me matam idam nityam anutishthanti maanavaah;

Shraddhaavanto'nasooyanto muchyante te'pi karmabhih.3-31

Explanation to Verse 3-31

ये – Those, मे – me, मतम् – teaching ,इदम्, this नित्यम्-constantly, अनुतिष्ठन्ति-practice, मानवाः- men श्रद्धावन्तः - filled with faith, अन-सूयन्तः - without being critical, मुच्यन्ते -freed ते –they, अपि –too, कर्मभिः from Karma

Those men who constantly practise my teaching with full faith and without being critical, they too are freed from actions.3-31

Commentary 3.31

Practice by repetition of any activity strengthens skills. At the same time, there must be 'Shradda' – faith in the activity to lead to expected results. A devotee who constantly practices Gita's teachings is bound to achieve freedom from the shackles of karma.

Verse 3-32

ये त्वेतदभ्यसूयन्तो नानुतिष्ठन्ति मे मतम् ।

सर्वज्ञानविमूढांस्तान्विद्धि नष्टानचेतसः ॥ ३-३२॥

Sandhi break-up

ये तु एतत् अभ्यसूयन्तः, न अनुतिष्ठन्ति मे मतम् ।

सर्वज्ञानविमूढान् तान्, विद्धि नष्टान् अचेतसः ॥

Ye twetad abhyasooyanto naanutishthanti me matam;
Sarvajnaanavimoodhaam staan viddhi nashtaan achetasah.3-32

Explanation to Verse 3-32

ये- those who, तु –but, एतत् – this, अभ्यसूयन्तः - carp (difficult to please), न अनुतिष्ठन्ति – do not practice, मे मतम्- my teaching, सर्वज्ञान विमूढान् – deluded in all knowledge, most foolish, तान् –them, विद्धि –know, नष्टान् , ruined, अचेतसः – devoid of discrimination

But those who carp (difficult to please, always criticize) at My teaching and do not practise it, deluded in all knowledge and devoid of discrimination, know them to be ruined. 3-32

Commentary 3-32

Knowledge should be used in an intelligent way. Fire can be used for cooking but carelessness and misuse can cause injury.

Verse 3-33

सदृशं चेष्टते स्वस्याः प्रकृतेर्ज्ञानवानपि ।

प्रकृतिं यान्ति भूतानि निग्रहः किं करिष्यति ॥ ३-३३॥

Sandhi break-up

सदृशं चेष्टते स्वस्याः, प्रकृतेः ज्ञानवान् अपि ।

प्रकृतिं यान्ति भूतानि, निग्रहः किं करिष्यति ॥

Sadrisham cheshtate swasyaah prakriter jnaanavaan api;
Prakritim yaanti bhootaani nigrahah kim karishyati.3-33

Explanation to Verse 3-33

सदृशं – in accordance, चेष्टते – acts, स्वस्याः – on his own, प्रकृतेः – of nature, ज्ञानवान् – a wise man, अपि even, प्रकृतिं – to nature, यान्ति – follow, भूतानि – living beings, निग्रहः:- restraints, किं – what, करिष्यति - will do

Even a wise man acts in accordance with his own nature; beings will follow nature; what can restraint do? 3-33

Commentary 3-33

Nature follows certain laws that cannot be changed. Some trees blossom only during certain times – sometimes once in twelve years! Likewise, human beings too act according to their nature following inborn qualities.

Verse 3-34

इन्द्रियस्येन्द्रियस्यार्थे रागद्वेषौ व्यवस्थितौ ।

तयोर्न वशमागच्छेत्तौ ह्यस्य परिपन्थिनौ ॥ ३-३४॥

Sandhi break-up

इन्द्रियस्य इन्द्रियस्य अर्थे, रागद्वेषौ व्यवस्थितौ ।

तयोः न वशमागच्छेत् तौ, हि अस्य परिपन्थिनौ

Indriyasyendriyasyaarthe, raagadweshau vyavasthitau;

Tayor na vasham aagacchet tau, hyasya paripanthinau. 3-34

Explanation to Verse 3-34

इन्द्रियस्य – of the senses, इन्द्रियस्य अर्थे, - in the sense objects, रागद्वेषौ – attachment and aversion, व्यवस्थितौ, exist, seated, तयोः – of these, न – never, वशम्- control, आगच्छेत् – come under, तौ,- those, हि , certainly, अस्य- his, परिपन्थिनौ- stumbling blocks, enemy

Attachment and aversion for the objects of the senses abide in the senses; let none come under their control, for they are certainly his foes.3-34

Commentary 3-34

Likes and dislikes are natural but one should not come under complete control of the senses for it leads to weakness.

Verse 3-35

श्रेयान्स्वधर्मो विगुणः परधर्मात्स्वनुष्ठितात् ।
स्वधर्मे निधनं श्रेयः परधर्मो भयावहः ॥ ३-३५॥

Sandhi break-up

श्रेयान् स्वधर्मः विगुणः परधर्मात् स्वनुष्ठितात् 1
स्वधर्मे निधनं श्रेयः परधर्मः भयावहः ॥

Shreyaan swadharmo vigunah paradharmaat swanushthitaat;
Swadharme nidhanam shreyah paradharmo bhayaavahah.3-35

Explanation to Verse 3-35

श्रेयान् – better, स्वधर्मः, one's own duty, विगुणः-devoid of merit, परधर्मात् – than the duty of another, स्वनुष्ठितात्- than well-performed, स्वधर्मे – in one's own duty, निधनं – death, श्रेयः – better, परधर्मः – another, भयावहः:- filled with fear.

Better is one's own duty, though devoid of merit, than the duty of another well discharged. Better is death in one's own duty; the duty of another is fraught with fear.3-35

Commentary 3-35

Following Swadharma or one's own duty is stressed by the Lord. A Cobbler by birth may be ill-fitting to do the work of a skilled plumber or carpenter. A brave soldier may be better suited to fight on the battlefield than a priest who performs Puja in a temple.

Abandoning one's duty and following another merely because of some attraction (like more salary or appeal of comfort and luxury) may be harmful to a person.

Verse 3-36

अर्जुन उवाच ।

अथ केन प्रयुक्तोऽयं पापं चरति पूरुषः ।

अनिच्छन्नपि वार्ष्णेय बलादिव नियोजितः ॥ ३-३६ ॥

Sandhi break-up

अथ केन प्रयुक्तः अयं, पापं चरति पूरुषः

अन्-इच्छन् अपि वार्ष्णेय, बलात् इव नि-योजितः

Arjuna Uvaacha:

Atha kena prayukto'yam paapam charati poorushah;

Anicchann api vaarshneya balaad iva niyojitah.3-36

Explanation to Verse 3-36

अथ – now, केन- by which, प्रयुक्तः – impelled, driven अयं-this, पापं –sin, चरति – does, commits, पूरुषः –man अन्-इच्छन् – not wishing, अपि – even, वार्ष्णेय,- O Varshneya (Krishna, of Vrishni race), बलात्- **by force**, इव- as it were, नि-योजितः:- constrained

Arjuna said:

O Varshneya (Krishna), But impelled by what does man commit sin, though against his wishes, constrained, as it were, by force? 3-36

Commentary 3-36

What is the force that impels a person to commit sin? The Lord answers this question in the next verse.

Verse 3-37

श्रीभगवानुवाच ।

काम एष क्रोध एष रजोगुणसमुद्भवः ।

महाशनो महापाप्मा विद्धेनमिह वैरिणम् ॥ ३-३७॥

Sandhi break-up

कामः+एषः क्रोधः+एषः (विसर्गसन्धिः), रजो-गुण-समुद्भवः

महा-अशन:+महापाप्मा, विद्धि + एनम् + इह वैरिणम्

Sri Bhagavaan Uvaacha:

Kaama esha krodha esha rajoguna samudbhavah;

Mahaashano mahaapaapmaa viddhyenam iha vairinam.3-37

Explanation to Verse 3-37

कामः – desire, एषः-this, क्रोधः- anger, एषः – this रजो-गुण-समुद्भवः: - born out of Rajo Guna, महा-अशन: - all-devouring, महापाप्मा, - all sinful, विद्धि- know, एनम् –this इह-here, वैरिणम् –the foe, enemy

The Blessed Lord said:

It is desire, it is anger born of the quality of Rajas, all-sinful and all-devouring; know this as the foe here (in this world).3-37

Commentary 3-37

The most powerful force in a person is desire. When this desire turns into anger or wrath, it becomes destructive. So, the root cause is really desire – a quality of Rajas.

Verse 3-38

धूमेनाव्रियते वह्निर्यथादर्शो मलेन च ।

यथोल्बेनावृतो गर्भस्तथा तेनेदमावृतम् ॥ ३-३८॥

Sandhi break-up

धूमेन आव्रियते वह्निः, यथा दर्शः मलेन च

यथा उल्बेन आवृतः गर्भः, तथा तेन इदम् आवृतम्

 Dhoomenaavriyate vahnir yathaadarsho malena cha;
Yatholbenaavrito garbhas tathaa tenedam aavritam.

Explanation to Verse 3-38

धूमेन – by smoke, आव्रियते – is enveloped, वह्निः – fire, यथा – as, आदर्शः- a mirror, मलेन – by dust (pollutant), च – and, यथा –as, उल्बेन – by the membrane, आवृतः- enveloped, गर्भः – embryo, तथा-so, तेन – by it, इदम् - this आवृतम् -enveloped.

As fire is enveloped by smoke, as a mirror by dust, and as an embryo by the membrane (amnion), so is this enveloped by that.3-38

Commentary 3-38

Desire is compared to smoke that envelops the fire. Blowing some air into the smoke (a common practice in rural India's kitchens) will clear the smoke and reveal the fire. The resplendent Atman like fire is veiled in the desire of smoke.

Verse 3-39

आवृतं ज्ञानमेतेन ज्ञानिनो नित्यवैरिणा ।

कामरूपेण कौन्तेय दुष्पूरेणानलेन च ॥ ३-३९॥

Sandhi break-up

आवृतं ज्ञानम् एतेन, ज्ञानिनः नित्यवैरिणा (नित्यं-वैरी-तेन) ।
कामरूपेण कौन्तेय दुष्पूरेण अनलेन च ॥

Aavritam jnaanam etena jnaanino nityavairinaa;
Kaamaroopena kaunteya dushpoorenaanalena cha.3-39

Explanation to Verse 3-39

आवृतं – enveloped, ज्ञानम् – wisdom, एतेन – by this, ज्ञानिनः-of the wise, नित्यवैरिणा – by the constant enemy, कामरूपेण – in the form of desire, कौन्तेय- O Kaunteya (Arjuna), दुष्पूरेण – insatiable, अनलेन –as fire च - and

O Arjuna, wisdom is enveloped by this constant enemy of the wise in the form of desire, which is insatiable as fire! 3-39

Commentary 3-39

The mind of a man moves away from the Lord clouded by the smoke of desires.

Verse 3-40

इन्द्रियाणि मनो बुद्धिरस्याधिष्ठानमुच्यते ।
एतैर्विमोहयत्येष ज्ञानमावृत्य देहिनम् ॥ ३-४० ॥

Sandhi break-up

इन्द्रियाणि मनः बुद्धिः, अस्य अधिष्ठानमुच्यते ।
एतैः विमोहयति एषः, ज्ञानम् आवृत्य देहिनम् ॥

Indriyaani mano buddhir asyaadhishthaanam uchyate;
Etair vimohayatyesha jnaanam aavritya dehinam.3-40

Explanation to Verse 3-40

इन्द्रियाणि – the senses, मनः – the mind, बुद्धिः – the intellect, अस्य – its, अधिष्ठान- seat, मुच्यते – is called, एतैः-by these, विमोहयति- deludes, एषः-this, ज्ञानम्- wisdom, आवृत्य – having enveloped, देहिनम् - the embodied.

The senses, the mind and the intellect are said to be its seat; through these it deludes the embodied (man) by veiling his wisdom. 3-40

Commentary 3-40

As Ramakrishna Paramahamsa said: "The mind directed to sensuous desires is like a holy man amongst bullies or like a wealthy man living in a slum."

Verse 3-41

तस्मात्त्वमिन्द्रियाण्यादौ नियम्य भरतर्षभ ।

पाप्मानं प्रजहि ह्येनं ज्ञानविज्ञाननाशनम् ॥ ३-४१ ॥

Sandhi break-up

तस्मात्-त्वम्-इन्द्रियाणि, आदौ नियम्य भरतर्षभ 1

पाप्मानं प्रजहि हि-एनं, ज्ञान-विज्ञान-नाशनम् ॥

Tasmaat twam indriyaanyaadau niyamya bharatarshabha;
Paapmaanam prajahi hyenam jnaana vijnaana naashanam.3-41

Explanation to Verse 3-41

तस्मात्- therefore, त्वम्- you, इन्द्रियाणि- the senses,आदौ-in the beginning, नियम्य – having controlled, भरतर्षभ – O' the best of the Bharatas (Arjuna), पाप्मानं – the sinful, प्रजहि-kill, हि-surely, एनं, this, ज्ञान-विज्ञान-नाशनम् - the destroyer of knowledge and realization.

Therefore, O best of the Bharatas (Arjuna), controlling the senses first, kill this sinful thing (desire), the destroyer of knowledge and realisation!3-41

Commentary 3-41

Conquer the senses and destroy desires to gain knowledge and realization.

Verse 3-42

इन्द्रियाणि पराण्याहुरिन्द्रियेभ्यः परं मनः ।

मनसस्तु परा बुद्धियों बुद्धेः परतस्तु सः ॥ ३-४२ ॥

Sandhi break-up

इन्द्रियाणि पराणि – आहुः, इन्द्रियेभ्यः परं मनः 1

मनसः- तु-परा –बुद्धिः, यः- बुद्धेः- परतः- तु सः ॥

Indriyaani paraanyaahur indriyebhyah param manah;

Manasastu paraa buddhir yo buddheh paratastu sah.3-42

Explanation to Verse 3-42

इन्द्रियाणि- the senses, पराणि – superior, आहुः:-they say, इन्द्रियेभ्यः:- than the senses, परं – superior, मनः – the mind, मनसः- than the mind तु-परा –बुद्धिः,- but, superior-intellect, यः:- **who** बुद्धेः:-than the intellect, परतः:- greater, तु –but सः:-He (Atman)

They say that the senses are superior (to the body); superior to the senses is the mind; superior to the mind is the intellect; and one who is superior even to the intellect is He—the Self.3-42

Commentary 3-42

Mind dominates over the senses and so it is superior to them. The Taittiriya Upanishad (2.1-5) describes that there are five sheaths (*pancha-koshas*) like onion peels that lead from the gross stage to the fine stage. They are:

Annamaya kosha, "food" sheath (Anna)

Pranamaya kosha, "energy" sheath (Prana)

Manomaya kosha "mind" sheath (Manas)

Vijñānmāyā kosha, "discernment" sheath (Vijnana)

Anandamaya kosha, "bliss" sheath (Ananda)

Knowing the subtle influences of the five elements within each kosha discerns the Self amidst appearances.

Verse 3-43

एवं बुद्धेः परं बुद्ध्वा संस्तभ्यात्मानमात्मना ।

जहि शत्रुं महाबाहो कामरूपं दुरासदम् ॥ ३-४३ ॥

Sandhi break-up

एवं बुद्धेः परं बुद्ध्वा संस्तभ्य आत्मानम् आत्मना ।

जहि शत्रुं महाबाहो कामरूपं दुरासदम् ॥

Evam buddheh param buddhwaa samstabhyaatmaanam aatmanaa;
Jahi shatrum mahaabaaho kaamaroopam
duraasadam.3-43

Explanation to Verse 3-43

एवं –Thus, बुद्धेः – than the intellect, परं-superior, बुद्ध्वा- having known, संस्तभ्य – restraining, आत्मानम् – the Self, आत्मना – by the Self, जहि – kill , शत्रुं – enemy, महाबाहो =महा (mighty, big)+ बाहो – (arms), O mighty-armed (Arjuna), कामरूपं = काम (desire)+ रूपं (form), in the form of desire, दुरासदम् – hard to conquer.

Thus, knowing Him who is superior to the intellect and restraining the self by the Self, kill, O mighty-armed Arjuna, the enemy in the form of desire, that is hard to conquer!3-43

Commentary 3-43

Most humans think foolishly that desires lead to happiness. Spiritual awakening leads to self-realization and desires automatically recede. Therefore, kill the enemy of desire.

5.1 Summary of Chapter 3

Arjuna is confused on knowledge and action. Asks Krishna which is better?

Krishna answers: Everyone is driven to action by the Gunas -Rajas, Tamas, and Sattwa.

One who engages himself in Karma Yoga without attachment, he excels!

Krishna doesn't advocate any form of renunciation of the material world.

Do your duty: Action is superior to inaction!

Explains Yagna-Sacrifice and the Cycle of Nature

Talks about a leader and how he sets a model for other people.

Explains the differences between a Gyaani and Agyaani - the wise and the ignorant

Recommends faith and surrendering all actions to Him

Arjuna asks Krishna what is the force that makes people committ sins.

Krishna names 'Kama Krodah' born of 'Rajas' and recommends control of senses to avoid sins.

5.2 Conclusion of Chapter 3

ॐ तत्सदिति श्रीमद्भगवद्गीतासूपनिषत्सु
ब्रह्मविद्यायां योगशास्त्रे श्रीकृष्णार्जुनसंवादे
कर्मयोगो नाम तृतीयोऽध्यायः ॥ ३॥

Hari Om Tat Sat Iti Srimad Bhagavadgeetaasoopanishatsu

Brahmavidyaayaam Yogashaastre Sri Krishnaarjunasamvaade

Karmayogo Naama Tritiyo'dhyaayah

(Sri Haraye Namah!)

Thus, in the *Upanishads* of the glorious *Bhagavad Gita,* the science of the Eternal, the scripture of Yoga, the dialogue between Sri Krishna and Arjuna, ends the third discourse entitled: **Karma Yoga- "The Yoga of Action"**

Conclusion

What does the Bhagavad Gita Teach Us?

We find joy in reading ancient Sanskrit terms that showcase its phonetic richness, root-based structure, aesthetic expression, and philosophical depth. Sanskrit conveys important ideas about decision-making, existence, and spirituality, especially in the Bhagavad Gita. This ancient text offers timeless insights and practical guidance for navigating life's complexities.

At its core, the Gita teaches the concept of 'Dharma,' or duty, illustrated by Arjuna's moral struggle on the battlefield, where Krishna advises him to fulfill his responsibilities. It encourages performing duties without attachment to outcomes, promoting inner peace in a fast-paced world.

The Gita also highlights the importance of self-realization and the pursuit of knowledge as paths to spiritual enlightenment, urging us to connect with our true nature. By overcoming self-doubt and recognizing the impermanence of the material world, we can face challenges with courage.

The Gita's teachings transcend cultural boundaries, offering practical wisdom for leading a meaningful and purposeful life.

Its teachings transcend cultures, providing practical wisdom for a meaningful life. Ultimately, the Gita serves as a guiding light for achieving balance and spiritual fulfillment.

Author's Appeal

While every effort has been made to ensure the accuracy of this book, some errors may have gone unnoticed. If you come across any inaccuracies or have suggestions for improvement, please don't hesitate to reach out to the author at gurujisubi@gmail.com. Your feedback is invaluable and will help enhance future editions.